D1826053

what would Jesus drive. . .

. . . and should you care?

what would
Jesus drive...

...and should
you care?

A look at what it

means to be Christian

in today's culture

JIM WILCOX

Beacon Hill Press of Kansas City
Kansas City, Missouri

Copyright 2004
By Jim Wilcox and Beacon Hill Press of Kansas City

ISBN 083-412-0968

Printed in the
United States of America

Cover design by Paul Franitza

Unless otherwise indicated all Scripture quotations are from the *Holy Bible, New International Version*® (NIV®). Copyright © 1973, 1978, 1984 by International Bible Society. Used by permission of Zondervan Publishing House. All rights reserved.

Scripture quotation marked KJV is from the King James Version.

Library of Congress Cataloging-in-Publication Data

Wilcox, Jim, 1952-
    What would Jesus drive— and should you care? : a look at what it means to be Christian in today's culture / Jim Wilcox.
        p. cm.
    ISBN 0-8341-2096-8 (pbk.)
    1. Jesus Christ—Ethics. 2. Christian ethics—Church of the Nazarene authors. I. Title.
    BS2417.E8W55 2004
    261'.0973—dc22

                                                        2003025798

10 9 8 7 6 5 4 3 2 1

contents

foreword

It is not without a significant amount of theological presumption that one begins an endeavor such as this, attempting to discern how Jesus Christ, the Son of God, would live in today's American culture. After all, He was both human being and divine being, both carpenter and nomad, both shepherd and rabbi. He spent a great deal more of His time ministering to others than He did taking care of himself, and His teachings indicate we are to do likewise, putting the needs and wants of others ahead of our own.

That's precisely what makes this task so difficult: Jesus would no more fit into American society today than He did into the Mediterranean culture of His time, which ultimately killed the Messenger because it couldn't tolerate His message.

If American media is both reflection and dictation of the direction of this culture, this is a most selfish country, based on radical individualism, rampant materialism, blind greed, and almost uncontrollable consumerism. Television, particularly, is little more than a massive marketplace that draws potential buyers with some of the most blatantly inane *entertainment* that has ever been broadcast. Interestingly, it is this secondary purpose of television, entertainment, that gets most of viewers' conscious attention, both positive and negative. When people, either individually or collectively, praise or criticize television, it is almost always the programming that draws most of the energy. Few viewers give due import to the message that is preached *between* those 10-minute segments of *Friends, Frasier,* or *Fear Factor,* the commercials that tell them what to eat, what to wear, what to drive, what to drink, or even what to watch next. Yet it is this high-tech, ear-catching, eye-popping, toe-tapping commercial-mania that seems to be having such a profound effect on what American consumers believe is imperative for their day-to-day living.

Let's face it: we have become obsessed with our *stuff*. We believe those advertisers when they tell us that we will "never get ahead" (wherever that is) until we start to "dress for success," drive the "ultimate driving machine," or retain the impossible appearance of perpetual youth and vigor. According to commercials, we should never have to suffer any physical pain, social rejection, emotional neglect, or psychological trauma. If we can simply take the newest medicine (and don't you just love all the side effects that are often worse than the original malady in the first place?), afford the latest fashion, be seen in the fanciest vehicle, marry the man or woman everyone else wanted to marry, work in the perfect career, live in the perfect neighborhood, even worship perfectly in the perfect church, our lives will be overwhelmingly fulfilling. Exciting and content. Perfect.

The fallout from this pervasive message—a message pounded into our spirits 3,000 times a day, according to media critics—is that we will never find that fulfillment, excitement, or contentment. As soon as we think that our garages are full of luxury, our closets full of affluence, and our stomachs full of Big Macs today, we are convinced by the media that we need more, better, and bigger, and we need it no later than tomorrow morning.

If you were to enjoy the "perfect day" as portrayed by today's commercials, you would wake up naturally (there are no alarm clocks in TV Utopia) to the aroma of the world's greatest coffee (stimulant included), eat various health foods that are at the same time calorie-free and life-affirming, surrounded by well-groomed and immaculately dressed, smiling children and a wife or husband fresh from the latest magazine cover. You would take your well-fed and perfectly clad body out to your swept and freshly painted suburban garage and find the world's finest automobile just waiting to take you in comfort to your high-paying and totally engrossing job, helping others while you earn seven figures. At noon, between having your nails filed and polished, your hair styled and colored, and your skin toned and tanned, you would eat a 325 fat-gram lunch, of which only 3 would actually be absorbed into your honed abdominal muscles. After an afternoon of self-fulfillment back at the feng-shuied office, you would head back to your plush green yards in your high-performance "driving machine," green lights and friendly police officers all the way.

At home you would find your spouse, even more attractive and youthful than when you left him or her eight hours ago, your kids, eager to tell you some of the most exciting news that you've ever heard, a dog with shiny coat and compassionate eyes, and a vibrating-drink-holding-reclining-hydraulic-surround-sound-reclining chair of Corinthian leather that actually revitalizes you more effectively than 12 hours of uninterrupted slumber. After dinner, the whole family would gather around the big-screen television set in your media room and all of you would enjoy the same program for the same reasons, nobody fighting over the remote or which chair to sit in. Before you know it, the kids have scampered voluntarily off to bed, homework completed (top of the class, your kids) and you're ready to climb into the firmest bed with the silkiest sheets ever made for the greatest night's rest any human being has ever had.

Yeah, I have that kind of day every day!

But that's exactly the type of lifestyle to which we feel entitled because we are tax-paying citizens in the wealthiest country the world has ever known. It is our birthright to be comfortable and cared for. Our culture's message is that we should accept nothing less.

That's why being a follower of Jesus, the Nazarene carpenter, is so revolutionary. And so, so difficult. He said, "Woe to you who are rich, for you have already received your comfort. Woe to you who are well fed now, for you will go hungry. Woe to you who laugh now, for you will mourn and weep. Woe to you when all men speak well of you, for that is how their fathers treated the false prophets" (Luke 6:24-26). In both word and deed, He turned the world's priorities upside down. "Blessed are you who are poor, for yours is the kingdom of God. Blessed are you who hunger now, for you will be satisfied. Blessed are you who weep now, for you will laugh. Blessed are you when men hate you, when they exclude you and insult you and reject your name as evil, because of the Son of Man" (vv. 20-22).

There will be times, therefore, that writing and reading about how Jesus would live, what He would eat, drive, read, where He would live, work, worship, whom He would marry, befriend, trust, or when He would laugh and cry might seem anti-American. That is not to suggest that this book will be unpatriotic or anticapitalistic; indeed, that is not its purpose at all. The intention of what follows is to try to discern how we might recognize Jesus were He to make America in the 21st century His home. Much of it will be re-searched and based on historical traditions and values; some will be theory and conjecture based on current trends and practices. Ultimately, it will reflect a sociological ap-proach to the gospel, particularly that ethos revealed in Je-sus' great Sermon on the Mount.

the sermon on the mount

Paraphrased by Jim Wilcox

Truly transformed are you who separate yourselves from your own desires in the cause of the Kingdom because you recognize that the hope of heaven is yours.

Truly transformed are you who grieve for a loved one lost because you realize my Spirit longs to wrap its arms around you tonight.

Truly transformed are you who seek to serve anyone whose need is greater than your own because I, in turn, will meet your every need.

Truly transformed are you whose spiritual appetite supersedes your physical desires because my banquet table is full and I'm holding a chair for you.

Truly transformed are you who forgive and forget, whose humility refuses to judge, because that will allow me one day to treat you likewise.

Truly transformed are you when your heart invades my Great Heart because only then will your mirror begin to reflect my image.

Truly transformed are you who resolve conflict, even if it means a painful compromise, because as a result, all who surround you will seek to follow you anywhere.

Truly transformed are you when being my disciple begins to discipline you because only then can you start to see life's journey through a telescope.

Truly transformed are you when you become the target of lies and rumors simply for following my footsteps because you cannot believe the nice things I have said about you here in heaven—just like I've said about Moses and Jonah and Daniel.

Salt is good stuff. It enhances flavor and preserves freshness. It transforms mediocre food into good-tasting food and good-tasting food into a grand feast, simply by highlighting and accentuating what was truly there all along. Here's the deal: as salt is to food, you are to those around you. Your most important purpose on earth is to make all those you encounter in life better through encouragement and instruction. If you don't do this, frankly, your life becomes meaningless.

Light makes darkness obsolete just like knowledge makes ignorance obsolete. And for crying out loud—who can dispel darkness and ignorance better than you? Nobody. Anybody who turns on a flashlight but then stands it on end so the bulb faces the tabletop is a fool. The light is rendered useless and the batteries go dead. What's the point? You need to turn on your flashlight and shine it directly into the darkness so that darkness is made obsolete and the path to heaven is made known.

A lot of what I say may sound as if it violates the law of Moses or other prophets—at least strays a bit from the way the law has been interpreted over the years. But I have come here today to fulfill the law and ensure that every bit of it is accomplished. After all, the Ten Commandments are huge and whoever violates them or leads others to violate them is condemned, plain and simple. But whoever upholds them and encourages others to obey them is truly awesome. The Pharisees pretend to be righteous, and the teachers they hire pay lip service to the law, but they are not going to enter the kingdom of God on mere pretense. That's the truth.

Case in point: the sixth commandment is all about killing another human being, a creature of the Almighty. We understand that one. But did you know that if you get angry with another person, if you spread vicious rumors about a person, if you assassinate someone's character through slander or cursing, you are also guilty of murder? Think about that the next time someone begins to gossip maliciously about someone to you. If you pass that gossip along, you are in real spiritual danger.

So here's the deal: if you're on your knees one night, praying, talking to your Heavenly Father, and suddenly you realize someone has a gripe against you or that you're holding a grudge against someone, you need to get up and make amends with that person. No matter what it takes—repaying a debt, saying you're sorry, or even turning yourself over to the civil authorities. How can you expect to talk to the Father if you can't even talk to your brothers and sisters?

The seventh commandment is about betraying the trust of a spouse by having sex with someone else; even if you're single and have sex with a married person, you've enabled that person to commit adultery, and that makes you guilty of adultery too. But did you know that if you even fantasize about a man or woman other than your spouse, you're just as guilty as if you had followed through with the physical act?

The fact of the matter is, God is interested in the purity of your heart and the righteousness of your motive just as much, if not more, than He is in the actions of your eyes or hands or any other body part. And you should think about that long and hard.

The fidelity of the marriage bed is metaphorical for the faithfulness of Jesus Christ to His bride, the Church. So divorce, though accepted by the world these days for any reason whatsoever, is limited in God's eyes to cases of adultery. Any other excuse is unacceptable to Him. Just as He would never separate himself from the Church except when the Church is unfaithful to Him, you should not separate yourselves from your spouses except when they are unfaithful to you.

Don't align yourselves with the world by swearing allegiance to it. Vowing this or that in the form of an oath to some club or political agenda will detract from your primary purpose of following God. And don't follow statements with phrases like, "Swear to God" or "As God is my witness." Those oaths trivialize the relationship God seeks to have with you. If your spiritual lives are honest and full of integrity, a simple yes or no will be sufficient.

Now this next one is hard because it goes against everything the world teaches you about being a strong man or an assertive woman. The world claims that Moses' law of "an eye for an eye, and tooth for tooth" is all the mercy one is required to show in life. But I want you to take it a step further: I'm asking you to be 100 percent merciful and not to resist evil people at all. In other words, if someone hits you, don't hit back as the world teaches in its television shows and movies. Vengeance is too easy and it's not Kingdom behavior. Not in the least. What I want you to do is to stand there and let him hit you again.

And if someone sues you, don't countersue. That's the world's response to everything: "Do unto others as they do unto you, and if you can, do it unto them before they do it unto you." That's not Kingdom behavior. Not at all. What I want you to do is to give the guy what he's suing you for and more.

If someone wants to take your car stereo, give him your car too. If someone wants to take your television set, give him the DVD player too. If someone wants to borrow your favorite sweater, let her. The sooner you realize that it's only "stuff," the better off you'll be.

When I told you to "Love your neighbor as yourself," I wasn't just blowing in the wind, my friends. I meant it. And if you love your car stereo or television or sweater or any other possession more than you allow yourself to love another human being, then you're worse off than I thought.

The world teaches "black and white" because that makes

decisions easy. The world says, "Either you're for us or you're against us." That's ridiculous and not Kingdom behavior. Your so-called enemies are my children, too, and I want you to love all my children, no matter what political people tell you. Pray for everyone, but pray especially for your enemies. It's easy as pie to love the people who love you back; what I want you to do is love those who don't love you back. In fact, I want you to love those who hate you back. That's what I do, and you're always asking, "What would Jesus do?" So do what I do—love without reservation or condition.

The kingdom of God is not about showmanship, friends; it's about humility. So don't go around, hamming it up for the camera when it comes to doing random acts of kindness. If you give to the needy, do it anonymously and quietly. Otherwise, it doesn't count. When you do good things simply for the recognition, that's all you're going to get. But if you want your Heavenly Father to take notice, do your kind acts so nobody knows where they came from.

It's the same with prayer. Don't make some big show of it, standing up in church just so you can be heard and applauded by those around you. "My, how that Harry can pray. So eloquent. So emotional. So beautiful." It's hard for God to hear such fine speeches. Instead, pray in the privacy of your own heart, in the secrecy of your own room. Now that's what God listens to.

And one more thing about prayer: verbosity is out; brevity is in. Here's an example of a really good prayer:
"Dear Heavenly Father,
the Sire of our spirits, who bore us, has nurtured us and now awaits us in His rich kingdom.
I can't tell You how close to You I feel at this precise moment.
In fact, my cares for and about myself pale when compared to my excitement,
my bliss in following where You lead me,
both now and forever.

All I ask is that my basic needs to live be met:
> a little food to eat,
> a few clothes to wear,
> and a safe place to sleep when I am weary.

Please forgive me, Father, when I begin to ask for too much,
for Your mercy and grace are enough to provide me everlasting life.
I promise to show all around me an equal measure of mercy and grace when I am asked.
And I will do so in Your name—not my own.
Father, the easy way is often so tempting:
> help me overcome,
> make me strong . . .
> and fervent
> and good.

Make me like You.
Because all that is created, all that is imagined, all that is possible is Yours
> from this day until there is no night.

Amen."

Forgiveness breeds forgiveness. If you forgive those who wrong you, God will forgive you. But if you hold onto your grudges against those who wrong you, God will not forgive you.

One more piece of advice about humility. There's been a lot made about fasting lately, especially as some form of losing weight. Forget all that. Fasting is about putting spiritual matters ahead of physical appetites, about seeing life through a telescope instead of a microscope. And because fasting is a spiritual act, you need to do it secretly. Don't let everyone know you're fasting, anymore than you let them know you're praying or you're doing random acts of kindness. Anything done with a "Look at me" attitude may be meaningful to the world, but it is meaningless to God.

Your culture is teaching you to grab all you can, earn all you can, save all you can, spend all you can, and to live as if your 75 years of life on earth is it. That is so shortsighted. Instead of wasting all your days on earth trying to make yourself more comfortable or powerful, you should invest your time and money in the future—the eternal future.

Give away all you can to those who need it even more than you do. Live humbly. Don't let fashion magazines or car salesmen tell you how to spend your money. Wear your clothes until you wear them out. Drive your car until it won't go another mile. With the money you save, you might be able to feed a family for a year. Or 10 years. Isn't that more noble?

You really have a choice here: serve yourself and make yourself look good *or* serve God by making others feel good. You can't have it both ways.

Once you begin to live this way, you will start to worry far less. You'll be able to sleep at night. Your days won't be so cluttered with "Me first" thinking. Fretting over what to eat, what to drink, what to wear is such a waste of precious time. God provides for birds and lilies and grass and all His other creatures. Why wouldn't He provide for you, His number one creation?

Spend your time seeking God's kingdom. Let tomorrow's worries take care of themselves.

Stop judging people; stop playing God. That's not Kingdom behavior. Who says your standards are The Standard, anyway? If you judge others harshly, you will be judged harshly by God, and that won't be pretty.

You waste so much time nitpicking others when you should be analyzing your own spirit and your own actions. If you were to wake up each morning and confess, "I am the chief of sinners. No one's sin is greater than my own," you might be a lot more forgiving and a lot less judgmental. The kingdom of God is not about "Whosoever won't"; it's about "Whosoever will." So stop checking everybody's spiritual ID at the door. Just make sure your own ID is in order.

Listen: your Heavenly Father loves you supremely. He would have sent His Son for only you, if you want to know the truth. If you need something, just ask and He will give it to you. Just seek His truth and you will find it. When you knock on His door, He will open it to you.

The Father is not out to trick anyone. He loves you more than your dad or mom loves you. If you asked your mom for a sandwich, she wouldn't give you a rock to eat. If you asked your dad to fry you up some catfish, he wouldn't give you fried rattlesnake. And your mom and dad aren't divine—they're human, with human limitations and human faults. But your Heavenly Father *is* divine, and His resources are unlimited and pure.

Here's the Law of Moses in a nutshell: do to and for others as you would have them do to and for you. It's that simple.

Obviously, this life I'm calling you to is not going to be easy, but as you're finding out, things that are easy are usually pretty temporary and awfully flimsy. Lots of people look for the easy way out, the most gain for the least pain. But the kingdom of God has a narrow gate and only a few of you will ultimately find it.

Be careful. There are a lot of loose cannons filling pulpits these days. But if you watch them carefully, you'll see that their actions away from the sanctuary don't measure up to the words they preach from the platform. They just don't walk the talk. Keep your eye on them; watch what happens to them in the long run. Oh sure, they might have a large following today and their church might be "The Happening Church" this week or "The Fad Fellowship" this month, but they will ultimately succumb to the temptations of pride and power.

Watch and learn.

Not everyone who claims God as his or her Lord will enter the Kingdom. Only those who do His will can enter through that narrow gate. Some will say, "But I went to church every week" or "I performed miracles" or "I did a good deed every day." I will look them in the eye and say, "I don't even know your name. Get away from me."

You ask, "What *is* your will for my life?" Here's God's will for your life: build your house on the rock solid foundation of His Word. That's it.

"But what career should I pursue? Whom should I marry? Where should I live?" you ask.

There you go, worrying about tomorrow again. Listen. God gave you special gifts when you were created. He wants some of you to teach, some of you to work on cars, some of you to nurse the sick, and some of you to bake bread. You know what your special gift is because it's the very thing you want to do, the very thing you're good at doing. Make a list of the three careers you would love most and start preparing for them today. Right now. Don't listen to outside voices—listen to that quiet voice from within yourself. God will open doors and close doors, and soon you will be doing the thing you were born to do.

And when it comes to marriage partners, marry the person you can't picture yourself living without, then treat him or her like that every day you have left. Just make sure he or she feels the same about you.

And when it comes to a place to live, follow your quiet voice. Live where you want to live and don't live somewhere you hate. Just know that God wants you to build His kingdom wherever you call home. He's much more concerned about the foundation of your home than He is about the bricks of the walls or the shingles of the roof or even how you earned the money to buy those bricks and shingles.

The home He is preparing for you in heaven is your ultimate home, after all.

Amen.

1—what would Jesus drive?

A Christian Response to Ecology and Responsible Environmentalism

The Scripture

In the beginning God created the heavens and the earth. Now the earth was formless and empty, darkness was over the surface of the deep, and the Spirit of God was hovering over the waters.

And God said, "Let there be light," and there was light. . . .

And God said, "Let there be an expanse between the waters to separate water from water." So God made the expanse and separated the water under the expanse from the water above it. . . .

And God said, "Let the water under the sky be gathered to one place, and let dry ground appear." And it was so. . . .

Then God said, "Let the land produce vegetation; seed-bearing plants and trees on the land that bear fruit with seed in it, according to their various kinds." And it was so. . . .

And God said, "Let there be lights in the expanse of the sky to separate the day from the night, and let them serve as signs to mark seasons and days and years, and let them be lights in the expanse of the sky to give light on the earth." And it was so. . . .

And God said, "Let the waters teem with living creatures, and let birds fly above the earth across the expanse of the sky." So God created the great creatures of the sea and every living and moving thing with which the water teems, according to their kinds, and every winged bird according to its kind. . . .

And God said, "Let the land produce living creatures according to their kinds: livestock, creatures that move along the ground, and wild animals, each according to its kind." And it was so. . . .

Then God said, "Let us make man in our image, in our likeness, and let them rule over the fish of the sea and the birds of the air, over livestock, over all the earth, and over all the creatures that move along the ground." So God created man . . .

God blessed them and said to them, "Be fruitful and increase in number; fill the earth and subdue it. Rule over the fish of the sea and the birds of the air and over every living creature that moves on the ground." . . .

God saw all that he had made, and it was very good (Gen. 1).

The Discussion

The idea of Jesus driving anything, actually, is rather absurd, but the metaphorical question has been around since the sports utility vehicle (SUV) became a top-selling model of automobile on the American road. Because SUV's typically achieve less than ideal gasoline-consumption levels (heretofore signified by mpg, or "miles per gallon"), environmentalists have become concerned that SUVs are polluting the air at a significantly higher rate than vehicles that achieve a more economical and ecologically friendly rate of miles per gallon.

According to U.S. government publications, the average mpg-rate for the SUV ranges from the 2003 Toyota Rav4 (four-cylinder, two-wheel drive) at 25 mpg in the city and 31 mpg on the highway, to several 2003 models that get only 10 mpg in the city and 13 mpg on the highway, including Chevrolet's Avalanche, Suburban, and Tahoe, as well as the GMC Yukon. The average for all SUVs is 15.5 mpg for city driving and 19.9 mpg for highway driving (www.fueleconomy.gov).

These figures compare to the **minicompact** average of 18.6 mpg (city) and 26.1 mpg (highway), topped by BMW's Mini-Cooper (28/37); the **subcompact** average of 23 mpg (city) and 30.7 mpg (highway), topped by the new VW Beetle (42/49); the **compact** average of 24.2 mpg (city) and 31.7 mpg (highway), topped by the VW Golf and Jetta (42/49); the **midsize** average of 18.9 mpg (city) and 25.8 mpg (highway), topped by the Honda Accord (26/34); and the **large car** average of 18.0 mpg (city) and 26.3 mpg (highway), topped by the Chevrolet Impala (21/32). Compared to **trucks,** the SUV fares slightly worse: the standard two-wheel-drive pickup averages 16.7 mpg (city) and 21.2 mpg (highway). **Minivans** average 18.3 mpg (city) and 24.7 mpg (highway) (www.fueleconomy.gov).

The largest source of pollution in the United States that destroys the ozone layer and, therefore, increases global warming is transportation, according to the *Evangelical Environment Network & Creation Care Magazine,* "and the United States is the world's largest emitter of greenhouse gases" (www.whatwouldjesusdrive.org). As the number of cars on the road today continues to rise, fuel economy is at a 22-year low, according to EEN&CCM.

Unfortunately, Americans can no longer isolate their opulent consumerism in this regard. As the ozone layer is depleted and the earth's atmosphere gets warmer, the spread of diseases like malaria will hit hardest in third world countries. This, then, becomes not just a health issue but a moral issue as well. Furthermore, not only is this pollution directly harming human beings, but plants and trees all over the world are becoming less and less capable of sustaining life. They are more vulnerable to pestilence and disease and less able to store nutrients.

When Jesus told His followers, "whatever you did for one of the least of these brothers of mine, you did for me," and "whatever you did not do for one of the least of these, you did not do for me" (Matt. 25:40 and 45), He was calling them (us) to a level of compassion that reaches around the globe. When we drive vehicles that do more than their fair share of polluting the air, we are not only destroying the future of our children and grandchildren but also destroying the lives of people we've never met in places we've never heard of.

Another side of this issue that many don't like to consider is the whole idea of modesty and humility. What we drive not only bears on what we breathe and drink and eat, or how hot the earth is getting, but it also goes a long way in telling those around us where our priorities lie. Writers like Ron Sider *(Rich Christians in a World of Hunger)* and Anthony Campolo *(Who Switched the Pricetags?* and *Twenty Hot Potatoes Christians Are Afraid to Touch)* have been asking Americans for years to think about social obscenities such as world hunger, abject poverty, homelessness, and catastrophic disease. Their question, "Would Jesus own a BMW?" seems a valid one to ask in this context. Should we spend more than we *need to* spend on a vehicle whose basic purpose is get us from point A to point B, when a car priced thousands of dollars less will do the very same thing? Are we that vain or insecure or just plain "uncomfortable" to think that what we drive really matters in God's divine plan?

What Jesus might recommend is for us to take the money we might have spent on a new luxury car and buy a used efficient car instead. Then, we could send the money we save on our status symbols to our local orphanages or homeless shelters or rescue missions. Or we might take that money we save and buy a vehicle for our church or a neighbor whose car never starts.

Campolo tells the story of being asked to pray at the end of a missions convention. One of the prayer requests was for God to supply a new utility vehicle for a young missionary couple whose car on the field had seen its last day. As Campolo bowed to pray, he felt compelled to raise his head and look at the vast crowd before him. Instead of praying, he said, "Why don't we become God's answer to prayer?" He asked everyone in the crowd to take out whatever cash he or she could find in his or her wallet, purse, and pocket and place it in the offering plates being circulated. In five minutes, they had collected more than enough funds to buy this godly couple a new car to use for His kingdom. That is how we should all feel about our cars—they are mere tools to build His kingdom.

As the United States becomes more and more dependent on foreign oil, U.S. national security becomes less and less stable. As the recent war with Iraq, the second-leading producer of crude oil in the world, demonstrates, our way of life is susceptible to the whims of politics. According to the Department of Energy (DOE), "two-thirds of the 20 million barrels of oil Americans use each day is used for transportation," and "half of the oil we use is imported—the highest level in U.S. history. Up to 75 percent of the world's oil reserves are in the Middle East and controlled by the members of the OPEC oil cartel" (www.whatwouldjesusdrive.org). Even before the war with Iraq, the United States was spending $40 billion a year to defend its oil interests in the region, according to the DOE.

The Bottom Line

Humorists all over the country have scoured the Scriptures to discover the exact model of automobile that Jesus would drive, and they've come up with some real finds. The psalmist suggests that Jesus might have preferred a Pontiac or Geo: "pursue [your enemies] with your *Tempest* and terrify them with your *Storm*" (83:15). Moses indicates in Exod. 19:13 that Jesus might have driven a Dodge pickup: "when the *Ram*'s horn sounds a long blast." Even Jesus himself alludes to His vehicle of choice in John's Gospel: "For I did not speak of my own *Accord*" (12:49) (www.highrock.com).

In Jesus' day, the common person's mode of transportation was the sandal, a thin piece of leather strapped onto each foot. People walked everywhere; of course, most lived their whole lives within a few miles of their birthplace, so walking was efficient and quite ecologically sound. There was little need or desire, for that matter, to head off into faraway countries to see what was on the other side of the hill. Farmers and others who could afford them usually had some sort of beast of burden: an ox or donkey or cow. At times, they could be harnessed to a two-wheeled cart to carry "passengers" from one end of the village to the other. For long distances, the camel was hard to beat, not only because of its long-legged gait but also for its ability to go long distances with little maintenance. But only the wealthy owned camels, kind of like today's luxury cars.

Many contend that Jesus would use mass transportation today and not drive any vehicle at all. That may indeed be true if He lived in a large city and had access to city buses, taxicabs, and carpools. If He lived in a rural community, however, He might drive a tractor or even ride a bicycle into town when He found himself running short on supplies. Of course, given the kind of lifestyle He led 2,000 years ago, it would be safe to suggest that He would walk most places.

One would certainly not violate the essence of the gospel by making any of the following changes in his or her lifestyle; in fact, one might even get closer to what Jesus would *really* do. First, whenever you can, walk. Walk to the local pharmacy to pick up your prescription, to the video store to return your rentals, to your job, to your church, to your school. Make walking more than mere exercise in the morning before work or in the evening after dinner. Actually choose to make walking your primary mode of transportation and use vehicles *only* when time or distance dictate. Of course, this will take some changes in schedules, perhaps forcing you to get up earlier or do several errands at once.

Second, buy a properly sized bicycle and put whatever money is left over into a comfortable seat. Face it, you won't ride it if it makes you hobble around for days afterward. There's no need to invest lots of money into cycling clothes or other doodads worn by the bike fanatics of your neighborhood; just a safety helmet and maybe a good-sized backpack will allow you to cut down on the amount of miles you drive your car or truck.

Meanwhile, write letters and make phone calls to your local legislators to begin building sidewalks and bike lanes in your community so that these responsible modes of transportation are safe and encouraged. Many states already make room for cyclists on the roads of their cities and towns, but far too many places are lagging way behind. It's also becoming quite common to squeeze sidewalks out of suburbia in order to build more homes per acre. That seems a real shame.

Third, become less independent on the road and more dependent on the transportation options available in your city. Again, this mandates a change in lifestyle, but if this country is going to get serious about the long-term damage it is doing to the environment, then all citizens will have to make some alternative plans. Take a bus or subway or rail wherever and whenever you can. Post the schedule on your refrigerator door and use whatever time you spend waiting reading a good book. Or better yet, writing one.

If your community doesn't have convenient mass transportation, consider forming a carpool for folks in your area who are heading in approximately the same direction at approximately the same time every day.

Fourth, think globally and long-term when you buy such things as lawn and recreational equipment. Most yards these days are not all that big, so instead of using a gas-powered lawn mower or edger, consider either electric or hand-powered equipment. The five-blade reel mowers used by our fathers and grandfathers (or mothers and grandmothers) are so much better than they used to be and cut a yard just as efficiently and beautifully as those seven-horse-power internal combustion monsters used by the macho men down the street. If the size of your yard or the condition of your health requires a gas-powered mower, at least you might consider sharing it with a neighbor or four, so instead of five mowers running for 2 hours a week, one mower can run for 10 hours a week.

Fifth, become actively opposed to industries that are guilty of deforestation, acid rain, nuclear waste, and other environmental abuses. Even writing letters and e-mails to those responsible or others who have power over these industries can become an effective tool for replenishing the planet and maintaining God's call to responsibly "rule over the fish of the sea and the birds of the air, over the livestock, over all the earth, and over all the creatures that move on the ground" (Gen. 1:26).

Finally, alternative fuels will be part of the long-term answer. Car manufacturers are already exploring the use of electricity to create hybrid cars that use less gas and oil. President Bush talked about exploring the use of hydrogen in future vehicles in his State of the Union address in January 2003. He got everyone's attention when he said the only byproduct dripping from the undercarriage of such a vehicle would be *water.*

Whatever Jesus would drive today, it's safe to assume that it would not call attention to itself, either due to its luxurious beauty and status or because of its horrible maintenance and appearance. According to His teaching and lifestyle in the Gospels, most likely He would drive a car that easily fit into His budget, was reliable and economical, and transported as many people as needed a ride that day. It would not be so fancy as to make His poor passengers uncomfortable, nor would it be so beat-up that His rich passengers refused to get in. And it would definitely be as harmless to the environment as He could find.

2—where would Jesus live?

A Christian Response to Neighborliness, Homelessness, and Family

The Scripture

"Everyone who hears these words of mine and puts them into practice is like a wise man who built his house on the rock. The rain came down, the streams rose, and the winds blew and beat against that house; yet it did not fall, because it had its foundation on the rock. But everyone who hears these words of mine and does not put them into practice is like a foolish man who built his house on sand. The rain came down, the streams rose, and the winds blew and beat against that house, and it fell with a great crash" (Matt. 7:24-27).

"Do not let your hearts be troubled. Trust in God; trust also in me. In my Father's house are many rooms; if it were not so, I would have told you. I am going there to prepare a place for you. And if I go and prepare a place for you, I will come back and take you to be with me that you also may be where I am. You know the way to the place where I am going. . . . I am the way and the truth and the life. No one comes to the Father except through me" (John 14:1-4, 6).

The Discussion

"Location, location, location"—what every real estate agent claims are the three most important things to consider when purchasing a home. Jesus echoes that same ideal when He speaks about our eternal home: "Location, location, location."

According to Scripture, we all have a choice to make

while we're living in our homes on earth: where do we want to spend the forevermore parts of our lives? If we build our houses on the sand of "serving mammon," our sentence will be "a great crash." If, however, we build our houses on the rock of God's salvation, our reward will be Paradise. Although this seems highly simplistic, given all the choices of a lifetime that are imbedded in each of these decisions, God's Word makes it that simple. "No one can serve two masters. Either he will hate the one and love the other, or he will be devoted to the one and despise the other. You cannot serve both God and money [mammon in KJV]" (Matt. 6:24).

Jesus seems much more concerned about *where God lives within our homes* than where our homes are actually located. Whether we live on a farm miles from the nearest town or in a high-rise apartment miles from the nearest farm, Jesus prays that our lives are so focused on serving God and other people that where we lay our heads at night is utterly secondary. He said in Matt. 8:20 and Luke 9:58: "Foxes have holes and birds of the air have nests, but the Son of Man has no place to lay his head."

So why do we put so much stress in our culture on our homes—the physical aspect of the "place to lay [our] heads"? It is the single most expensive decision we make, and even when the decision has been made, we spend great amounts of money maintaining, decorating, and furnishing our homes. According to two different studies, the median cost of owning a home in America ranges from $195,000 (www.huduser.org) to $265,000 over a 30-year mortgage (United States Census Bureau). Even for a house priced under $100,000 at an extremely low interest rate (5.65 percent), the homeowner will eventually pay over $250,000.

The United States Department of Housing and Urban Development reports in its 1999 findings that as many Americans (just under 10 million houses) paid from $100 to $199 a month for their mortgages as those who paid $500 to $599 or $800 to $899 a month. Most of today's houses were built between 1950 and 1979, peaking at 16,000,000 houses built in the 1960s. According to other demographic figures, most people live in suburban America, and there are significantly more homes in the South than in the Northeast, the Midwest, or the West (www.huduser.org).

On the other side of this ledger, of course, is the growing population of people in this nation who have no home at all. The Urban Institute estimates that 3.5 million people in the United States are homeless, and tragically, more than one-third (39 percent) of those are children. These numbers have nearly tripled over the past two decades. According to the National Coalition for the Homeless, "a person is considered homeless who lacks a fixed, regular, or adequate night-time residence, and has [either] a primary night-time residence that is a supervised public or private shelter, or an institution that provides a temporary residence, or a public or private place not designed as a regular sleeping accommodation for human beings" (www.nationalhomeless.org).

Single men comprise the largest group of homeless people (40 percent) while only 14 percent of the homeless population is single women. The 2001 U.S. Conference of Mayors found that family units are the fastest growing group of homeless, reaching 40 percent in the 27 cities reporting. Fifty percent of all homeless people are African-American, 35 percent are Caucasian, 12 percent are Hispanic, 2 percent are Native American, and 1 percent are Asian-American, according to the U.S. Conference of Mayors (www.nationalhomeless.org).

Poverty, of course, is cited by most reports as the primary reason so many people are out on the streets. In 2000, over 31 million people lived in poverty, which means they had to give up most of what we consider to be necessities, including a place to "lay their heads." One reason for this is that while the rich have been getting richer, the poor have been getting poorer. Minimum wage, though higher than it was 25 years ago, is actually worth over 18 percent *less* than it was then, due to inflation, according to the book, *The State of Working America* (Mishel, Bernstein, and Schmitt, 1999, from the Economic Policy Institute). Nowhere in the United States can a person afford even a small apartment when earning only minimum wage, unless he or she works 90 hours a week.

Furthermore, state and federal government programs of assistance to low-income people have decreased over the past decade. The "Aid to Families with Dependent Children" was repealed in 1996 and replaced with the "Temporary Assistance to Needy Families" program, but even with food stamps, this program cannot keep people above state poverty levels. "In the Institute for Children and Poverty study [2001], 37 percent of homeless families had their welfare benefits reduced or cut in the last year" (quoted at www.nationalhomeless.org).

Other factors that lead to homelessness are the current decreases in affordable housing units, lack of affordable health care, domestic violence, mental illness, and drug addictions. One in four homeless single adults suffers from some sort of mental illness that prevents him or her from taking care of himself or herself, maintaining a home, or remaining employed. This, of course, compounds the problem because poor people can't afford the medical assistance they need. It's a Catch-22 of horrific proportions. "Homeless people are far more likely to suffer from chronic health problems . . . such as tuberculosis, HIV/AIDS, diabetes, hypertension," and more. Others suffer from the effects of being homeless: frostbite, leg ulcers, upper respiratory infections, muggings, rape, lack of first aid, and lack of basic clean facilities (www.nationalhomeless.org).

All of this weighs heavily on the heart of Jesus because, you see, He, too, was homeless. He would, today, be an advocate for the rights of the homeless: the right to an education, the right to vote, the right to a livable income, the right to health care, even the right to live on the street without being thrown in jail. According to a 2002 study by the National Coalition for the Homeless, 80 percent of communities have laws that prevent anyone from living on the street, but 100 of those same communities lack enough shelter beds to accommodate their homeless population. Interestingly, according to this same study, it costs more to put these people through the legal system than it does to build shelters for them. Some communities are using tax money to make park benches too uncomfortable for anyone to recline on them (www.nationalhomeless.org).

One of the most telling statements made by a homeless person came after he was asked what he needed most. His response had nothing to do with a good meal or a new coat. He said the most desired blessing by *all* homeless people is a "good night's sleep." Because of the fear of being robbed or beaten or hustled off to jail, homeless people are never able to completely let go of consciousness; they hover on the edge of sleep, but never fully give in.

Is it any wonder, then, that Jesus put so much emphasis on the way all of us should treat our neighbors, if we're lucky enough, that is, to have a neighbor *next door?* A lot of effort and money are invested in keeping our next-door neighbors out of our yards and off our property. Fences, alone, cost hundreds of dollars to erect and more annual costs to maintain. Robert Frost's poem "Mending Wall" conveys the irony of helping a neighbor build a fence to keep the established border between properties visible and legal. He concludes what we've all come to expect in our neighborhoods: fences make for "good neighbors."

We're very territorial, we are. We have fences and hedges and tree-lines around our homes; we have alarms and bars and locks on our windows and doors; we have neighborhood guards and gossips (we call it Neighborhood Watch) patrolling our communities; we even have garage door openers that allow us to transition from inside to outside and outside to inside without ever being seen by anyone who lives near us.

While some of us have gone out and bought a "serious guard dog" to protect all of our stuff from being stolen, others of us have gone so far as to purchase a gun, presumably to shoot anyone who tries to take what belongs to us.

We have bought into the notion (some call it the American Dream) that our homes are, indeed, our castles, and "you'd better bring a small army with you, chump, if you plan to take any of it from me." We've dubbed it the *Make My Day* law.

Where is the admonition of Christ: "Do not resist an evil person. . . . If someone wants to . . . take your tunic, let him have your cloak as well. . . . Love your enemies and pray for those who persecute you. . . . Do not store up for yourselves treasures on earth . . . where thieves break in and steal" (Matt. 5:39-40, 44; 6:19)? According to Jesus, our homes are *not* our castles; our castles are in heaven, and it would behoove all of us to make sure we're sending enough money up there to build it.

The Bottom Line

The story goes that a rich man went to heaven and was being led through some of the most glorious neighborhoods he had ever seen. The homes were magnificent, more than he ever dreamed of when he was alive. That's why he was astonished to see his housemaid of 36 years, standing in the front yard of one of these mansions.

"Hey, Mr. Dalton," she yelled across the way. "I'm so glad to see you again."

"Yeah, Maria," he said, "nice to see you again, too."

He was much more excited to see what awaited him than he was in seeing a former employee. *If lowly Maria got a mansion like that, I can't wait to lay my eyes on my place. It will take my breath away.*

But as the walk continued, the mansions became smaller

and smaller, until many of them began to look like tract homes. But Mr. Dalton's walk didn't stop there. He was guided into a neighborhood of mere shacks, really, no more than four walls and a roof.

"Wait a minute," he complained to his guide. "This hut can't be for me. I had a great big house down there and I just saw Maria's huge mansion. If she gets that kind of place, why don't I get something at least that nice?"

"Mr. Dalton," the guide said sadly, "Maria spent her life sending us money through her church work, her contributions to local schools, her charities. You didn't pay her much, but she gave a lot of what you did pay her to other people. And that's how we got it.

"You, however, kept most of your abundant wealth for yourself, buying house after house, car after car, and you seemed pretty tightfisted when kids came by your front door, looking for money to support a school project or a mission trip.

"We did our best, Mr. Dalton, with what you sent us, but I'm afraid this is all we could afford to prepare for you."

It is safe to say that Jesus would today live with the homeless people of His community. That is not to suggest that He would judge anyone harshly for living in a nice house, but He would certainly expect those of us who do own nice houses to help support those who don't and can't. The Early Church was characterized by the concept of collecting the wealth of its people and redistributing it equitably. We do not earn what we earn in the workplace to spend it all at our own home place; we are instructed by Christ to give what we earn to as many people as we can, "and all these things shall be added unto you" (Matt. 6:33, KJV).

3—where would Jesus work?

A Christian Response to "Job," "Career," and "Mission"

The Scripture

For the kingdom of heaven is like a landowner who went out early in the morning to hire men to work in his vineyard. He agreed to pay them a denarius for the day and sent them into his vineyard.

About the third hour he went out and saw others standing in the marketplace doing nothing. He told them, "You also go and work in my vineyard, and I will pay you whatever is right." So they went.

He went out again about the sixth hour and the ninth hour and did the same thing. About the eleventh hour he went out and found still others standing around. He asked them, "Why have you been standing here all day long doing nothing?"

"Because no one has hired us," they answered.

He said to them, "You also go and work in my vineyard."

When evening came, the owner of the vineyard said to his foreman, "Call the workers and pay them their wages, beginning with the last ones hired and going on to the first."

The workers who were hired about the eleventh hour came and each received a denarius. So when those came who were hired first, they expected to receive more. But each one of them also received a denarius. When they received it, they began to grumble against the landowner. "These men who were hired last worked only one hour," they said, "and you have made them equal to us who have borne the burden of the work and the heat of the day."

But he answered one of them, "Friend, I am not being unfair to you. Didn't you agree to work for a denarius? Take your pay and go. I want to give the man who was hired last the same as I gave you. Don't I have the right to do what I want with my own money? Or are you envious because I am generous?"

So the last will be first, and the first will be last (Matt. 20:1-16).

The Discussion

One of the most common complaints about anyone's workplace is its apparent, if not blatant, unfairness. You can hear it all the time if you really want to; from the break room to the boardroom, everybody seems to think every now and then that he or she is getting cheated.

"They don't pay me enough!" "They want me to work all the time!" "That new guy's taking most of my clients away from me!" "Well, who died and made her Queen for the Day?"

Formal complaints made in the workplace range from discrimination to harassment, from safety concerns to loss of benefits. But some complaints seem to come under the umbrella of "personal preferences" rather than serious problems.

One in three workers gets so frustrated with colleagues' habits, including their shouting at computers, that he or she often wants to quit his or her job, according to a new survey.

A poll of 1,500 British workers by [the] recruitment firm, Office Angels, found the biggest complaints were about noise levels and technology on the job.

The most annoying habits of coworkers are listening to voice-mail messages on speaker phones, swearing at their computers, and refusing to pitch in with tea-making duties.

Nearly all respondents hated being sent an e-mail by someone sitting only a few feet away.

Two other big irritants? Workers who shout into the phone and people jamming the photocopier and leaving it for someone else to fix (www.cnn.com).

Jesus would probably be quite concerned about the more serious situations at one's workplace: certainly, He would seek *justice* at work when it comes to issues like safety and harassment and benefits, but He probably would preach *mercy* and *forgiveness* and *patience* in terms of some of these personal annoyances. Don't you think?

Christ's parable about the vineyard and the workers is full of wise counsel for anyone who works with other people. The message is quite clear: "Stop whining!" It is American culture that teaches all of us to equate the idea of fairness with our concepts of individualism, even to the point of selfishness. We're told from early on to stand up for ourselves, sell ourselves, make sure we get an equal slice of the pie. Terms like "justice" and "fairness," then, seem to go only as far as our own little cubicles. Can any of us imagine how Jesus' words would go over at most jobs today?

"OK, Bert. We're gonna start you off at $35,000 a year, base salary, and then you can earn as much from commissions as you want. Here's your contract to sign. Think it over and come see me tomorrow."

When Bert comes in the next day to hand in his signed contract, he sees a new guy sitting across from the boss and leans his good ear toward the door to hear what's going on.

"Hey, Butch. Good to see you this morning. I'd like to offer you a contract for $45,000 a year, and then you can earn as much money from commissions as you want. Here's a contract for you to look over tonight."

Six months later, the boss hires another salesman and gives him $40,000 to work only the last six months of the model year, plus commissions.

Wouldn't most workers call such dealings unfair? Jesus brings a whole new definition to the concept of fairness.

You should have heard the rumblings about fairness at the workplace several years ago when Anthony Campolo, a writer/speaker/professor/sociologist/philanthropist of some renown, suggested at a university faculty meeting that the young, new professors on campus should be paid the larger salaries because they had families to raise, mortgages to pay, mouths to feed. The professors who had been around for 30 or 40 years, who had already raised their families and paid off their mortgages, should be at the bottom of the pay scale, according to Campolo, because they, frankly, didn't need as much to live on. Does that sound fair? It sure did to those young, new professors who were there that day.

Many sermons have explicated this passage from Matthew on a much more spiritual level, and so they should. In the context of Jesus' teaching here, He is, indeed, alluding to the "spiritual fairness" of the kingdom of God: those who serve God all of their lives will reap the same reward of eternal life as those who come into the flock at the end of their lives. God doesn't play favorites, though many folk sure seem to think He does from time to time.

Have you ever heard anyone ask God, "Why me?" or "Why *not* me?" How about, "I go to church every Sunday and drive an old, beat-up Dodge; why does that guy who uses the Lord's name in vain every other word drive a brand-new Porsche?" Or maybe, "I don't drink or smoke or eat too much, but I get cancer. Those people across the street do all those things but will probably live to be 100!" Yep. We wonder about spiritual fairness all the time.

So the literal application to our behavior at work seems quite relevant as well: Jesus may have been telling us that we should keep our eyes on our own paychecks at the end of the day, week, or month, and not worry what the other guy at the other end of the line is earning. Life is just a whole lot simpler that way. Fairness is much easier to find.

Too many people hate their jobs. For any number of reasons, they just can barely get out of bed in the morning to go to work. The job may pay OK, but the traffic to and from work is unbearable. Or the job might be really close to home, just around the corner as a matter of fact, but the boss is super hard to get along with. Or the boss might be an angel straight from heaven but the actual work is *so boring*. Whatever. It seems tragic that these same people remain tethered to their horrible jobs because "It's the only thing I know"; or "I could never make that kind of money anywhere else"; or "Start over at the bottom? Are you kidding me?" And so every stinking day for 40 years, they go to jobs they despise, sit there and wonder why their lives are so stressed or their marriages are so drained or their kids don't speak to them.

What a waste of life, huh?

For the many, there is a hardly concealed discontent. The blue-collar blues is no more bitterly sung than the white-collar moan. "I'm a machine," says the spot-welder. "I'm caged," says the bank teller, and echoes the hotel clerk. "I'm a mule," says the steelworker. "A monkey can do what I do," says the receptionist. "I'm less than a farm implement," says the migrant worker. "I'm an object," says the high-fashion model (Studs Terkel, *Working*, xi-xii).

To these people we should say, "Make a list of the three things you love to do most. It doesn't matter how little you think it would *pay* or how much *time* it would take to get there. Just make the list. What do you want to do so much you can't even think straight?" And then once they make their list, we should tell them, "Now—*now*—go do those things."

When I was at a crossroads in my life, my roommate's brother came over to the couch where I was reading British poetry for a course I was taking, and we began to talk. It was he who gave me this advice: make a list of the things I enjoy doing most. So I sat there for several minutes, fantasizing about my life as a professional comedian. "I really like to make people laugh," I told him. Then I remembered all those years I spent with my radio on STUN and wrote down, "a rock and roll singer." But then I remembered how much I love to write, so I jotted, "the editor of a small-town weekly newspaper."

"Now—*now*—go after those!" he said.

It would be fun to share with you about my lucrative career as Jerry Seinfeld or Rod Stewart or Ben Bradlee, but I'm not any of those guys. Nope. I'm a professor at a small private school out in the relative middle of nowhere. A professor who is the adviser of our small campus weekly newspaper. A professor who gets to perform my own whacky kind of music at campus variety shows. A professor who has two or three or four captive audiences every day to survive my sense of humor. In other words, I'm a funny rock star who helps publish a newspaper. Whoa!

See, there's a big difference between a *job* and a *career.* It's much more than the old homily: "a job pays wages; a career pays a salary." In truth, a job is what puts food on the table, but a career puts a smile on your face. A job is where you put in your time, but a career is where you put your energy.

There are, of course, the happy few who savor their daily jobs: the Indiana stonemason who looks upon his work and sees that it is good; the Chicago piano tuner who seeks and finds the sound that delights; the bookbinder who saves a piece of history; the Brooklyn fireman who saves a piece of life. But don't these satisfactions, like Jude's hunger for knowledge, tell us more about the person than about his task? (Studs Terkel, *Working,* xi).

Jesus wants us to take the idea of work one step further. He said, "Seek first his kingdom and his righteousness, and all these things will be given to you as well" (Matt. 6:33). He also said, "Make disciples" (28:19). He turned the Great Commission into the "Great, come mission!" When our workplace becomes fertile soil for the mustard seed of the gospel, our careers become *missions*. And whether we are mechanics or manufacturers, plumbers or painters or police officers, teachers or technicians, we instantly become Great Commissionaries when we seek to make disciples of our coworkers. Our work becomes *His work.*

The Bottom Line

There is, today, a tremendously powerful idea in our culture called the work ethic. It says that work alone is what is valuable; in other words, people are valuable because they work. The converse is, of course, that people who don't work are not valuable. We have taken this to its absurd end—the more we work, the more valuable we become, so we have developed another powerful idea in our culture called workaholism. This is characterized by 15-hour days on the job, six or seven days a week, 50 to 52 weeks a year. It's also characterized by divorce, alienated kids, heart attacks, and suicide.

In everything He did, Jesus sought balance, and with this balance comes contentment. The Bible never calls us to give our lives to our jobs, even if we are pastors of the fastest-growing congregations in town or the only one in the church who can carry a tune. If our work starts to dominate our schedules, nay, our lives, we haven't understood that Jesus balanced His great acts of ministry with a lot of downtime to renew, refresh, and relax.

Nearly every story in the four Gospels is preceded or followed by Jesus' departures from the crowds, His sojourns to the other side of the lake. He needed time to pray and think and reconnect with the Twelve.

Jesus would work today in places where He could find that balance, where creativity brought as much reward as productivity. He would work in a place that brought contentment to His spirit, a place He couldn't wait to get to most mornings, a place of purpose and mission. Literalists will insist that He would be a carpenter today, and there's no reason to doubt that theory, but we certainly shouldn't limit Him to that one career choice. I mean, really! He is the Son of God, after all, and who are we to tell Him He can be only a carpenter?

Jesus would also work in an environment of mutual respect, where men and women were treated equally and fairly, where people of all colors worked side by side with each other, where employees' medical needs were compensated, where time away from work was expected and encouraged, where the ecology was revered, where children were taken care of on-site, and where bosses pulled their employees rather than pushed them.

After all, on His list of favorite things to do must have been "Heal, feed, and forgive."

4—what would Jesus wear?

A Christian Response to Wealth, Fashion, and Consumerism

The Scripture

While Jesus was in Bethany in the home of a man known as Simon the Leper, a woman came to him with an alabaster jar of very expensive perfume, which she poured on his head as he was reclining at the table.

When the disciples saw this, they were indignant. "Why this waste?" they asked. "This perfume could have been sold at a high price and the money given to the poor."

Aware of this, Jesus said to them, "Why are you bothering this woman? She has done a beautiful thing to me. The poor you will always have with you, but you will not always have me. When she poured this perfume on my body, she did it to prepare me for burial. I tell you the truth, wherever this gospel is preached throughout the world, what she has done will also be told, in memory of her" (Matt. 26:6-13).

The Discussion

This question, "What would Jesus wear?" is much like the question, "What would Jesus drive?" as far as status is concerned. Typically, both questions are asked by those who can't afford the BMWs and Rolexes, sometimes hoping that the implication of condemnation of those who can will *even the score* somehow. The problem with this sort of reasoning, however, is that Jesus was never concerned about *evening the score,* which carries the idea of vengeance; He was interested in simple justice.

45

Economic equality is an impossibility in this life. Even Jesus himself acknowledged this when He reacted to the woman who had poured expensive perfume on His feet: "The poor you will always have with you" (Matt. 26:11). But He prorated the standard of expectations, if you will, when in Luke 12 He said, "From everyone who has been given much, much will be demanded; and from the one who has been entrusted with much, much more will be asked" (v. 48). In other words, the poor and rich alike are asked to give to God's kingdom, but obviously the rich will actually give more gross wealth because they have more. Jesus was always more concerned about the spirit of the heart than the wad in the wallet, however, so the comparatively meager gift of the poor has an equal place of honor in the Kingdom:

Jesus sat down opposite the place where the offerings were put and watched the crowd putting its money into the temple treasury. Many rich people threw in large amounts. But a poor widow came and put in two very small copper coins, worth only a fraction of a penny.

Calling his disciples to him, Jesus said, "I tell you the truth, this poor widow has put more into the treasury than all the others. They all gave out of their wealth; but she, out of her poverty, put in everything—all she had to live on" *(Mark 12:41-44).*

When the rich man asked Jesus how he might inherit the Kingdom, Jesus told him to sell everything he had and give it to the poor. In this story, not only was Jesus demonstrating that God and money cannot both be worshiped; He was also describing the Kingdom as a place where words like "wealth" and "poverty" don't exist. In the eternal Kingdom, it really doesn't matter what kind of stuff you have in the temporal kingdom of this world. "Do not store up for yourselves treasures on earth where moth and rust destroy, and where thieves break in and steal. But store up for yourselves treasures in heaven, where moth and rust do not destroy, and where thieves do not break in and steal. For where your treasure is, there your heart will be also" (Matt. 6:19-21).

There's a poignant joke going around these days about a rich guy who died and was a bit disappointed in what he saw in heaven. At the gate, he asked the gatekeeper if he might be allowed to sneak back down to earth for just a minute and pick up a few things to bring back with him.

"I'm sorry, sir," the gatekeeper said. "Once here, I'm afraid it's permanent."

"Please, oh, please," begged the rich man, "I need just a couple of things from my life on earth. Just two, then I'll come right back."

Again, the gatekeeper told him that was not allowed.

"Please," the rich man cried again, "I'll bring just one thing back. Just one thing. Please let me go get just one thing and bring it up here."

Finally, seeing the desperation on the man's face, the gatekeeper relented and let him return to earth for one thing.

A few minutes later, the man, who had been quite wealthy in life, arrived back at heaven's gate with a truck-load of gold, shimmering beautifully in the celestial light.

The gatekeeper looked at the gold, then looked at the man and said. "Pavement? You wanted to bring back pavement?"

Walter Wangerin Jr. describes what the men of Jesus' day probably wore in his paraphrase of the Bible, *The Book of God: The Bible as a Novel:* "Joseph . . . was wearing a clean tunic of coarse woolen weave—sleeveless, roped at the waist, a blue stripe running down its right side from the shoulder to the hem. Over the tunic he had cast a cloak with loose blue fringes at each corner. His hair was oiled. His beard remained a thicket as high as his eyes, but the ends had been trimmed" (567).

This "outfit" is supported by Jesus in the great Sermon on the Mount, when He describes how His followers should treat each other. "And if someone wants to sue you and take your tunic, let him have your cloak as well" (Matt. 5:40).

A tunic is a loose-fitting garment that comes down to the knees or maybe slightly below the knees. Today, as with most clothing, it seems, tunics (which are still manufactured, purchased, and worn) are made out of cotton or man-made fabrics, but the people of Jesus' time were limited to what they could make from the animals they raised. The wool from sheep was most practical because it could be harvested without permanent damage to the animal. For the tunic, the material would have been loosely woven to allow air to circulate and keep the body as cool as possible. The cloak, on the other hand, was used to keep the body warm and would have been more tightly woven and much thicker. It would have been the more expensive item because of this.

On His feet, Jesus more than likely wore a modest sandal made from leather and fiber or other plant derivative that could be woven into straps. For those who could afford them, some sandals were made entirely of leather, both sole and strap.

The wealthy men of that day wore beautiful robes that were dyed with bright colors. Joseph of the Old Testament had a coat of many colors; some even suggest it had threads of gold woven through it. The footwear of the wealthy would have been ornate leather with gemstones occasionally woven into the sandals' straps.

On the head, status could also be worn. While villagers tended to clean their hair in the streams or lakes nearby, then apply oil to their locks to somehow make them manageable in the desert winds as well as make their heads somewhat aromatic, those in more urban areas, including the rich, wore turbans on their heads, their hair tucked neatly underneath. Again, these were often dyed and bejeweled to show the wearer's position in the community.

For most people, then, clothes were simply practical garments designed simply to permit modesty in mixed company and comfort in different climates. For a few, however, clothes became symbols of their wealth and status.

Honestly, it's not that different today, is it? Clothes still serve the dual purposes of function and fashion. Today, however, the fashion industry is the fourth largest industry in the world, raking in profits in the tens of billions of dollars, and Americans have become nearly obsessed with what they wear. Advertising plays a significant role in American consumer habits, and fashion is right near the top of what is advertised in the media.

Young people are particularly vulnerable to the whims—and costs—of fashion and its advertising because fitting in is the top priority of every teen in the country. Consequently, fashion malls have become the number one hangout of the adolescent culture; merchandisers and retailers have discovered that teens are among the very richest in the nation these days when it comes to discretionary funds, what one might call "leisure loot." Ask any teenager what he or she would do if handed $200, and 9 times out of 10, the answer will be, "Go to the mall, dude."

This phenomenon is most easily seen in the athletic shoe industry. Just a generation ago, tennis shoes, as they were called back then even though they were rarely worn to play actual tennis, were some of the least expensive shoes on the market. Made from canvas with rubber soles and simple dyes, they were relegated to the baseball field and basketball court. Most brands (and there were only three or four) cost less than $20 a pair.

Today, the tennis shoe is easily the biggest symbol of status in pop culture. Ranging from cross-trainers to walking shoes to court shoes to running shoes and more, these bad boys can run upwards of $200. They come in every color imaginable and are made mostly of leather and rubber.

Nike, the top seller in athletic shoes (Adidas is a climbing second), rakes in over $10 billion annually, with some of today's biggest names endorsing their products, including Michael Jordan, who has had his own line of Nike shoes for well over a decade.

For the older consumer, jewelry is what dazzles in the store window. Grooms-to-be feel compelled these days to show how much they love their brides-to-be with the size of the diamonds they intend to place on the women's fingers. It's almost become a competition on some university campuses, and many young couples are starting their marriages deep in debt because they have been suckered into thinking that the size of the "rock" correlates to the depth of the love. The fact of the matter is, diamonds are some of the most available gemstones in the world, but one company holds most of those diamonds in reserve and runs the prices up by controlling the market. Some critics of that company have even suggested that diamonds are so plentiful, the carbon from which they are derived is worth more than the stones themselves.

But does that matter? It doesn't seem to. Americans were among the top contributors to the industry's $8 billion in revenues in 2002. And it's not just rings: it's watches and necklaces and earrings too. Several years ago, Ray Stevens, a country-western humorist and songwriter, penned the song, "Would Jesus Wear a Rolex?" a song that indicts the televangelism medium for the hypocrisy of asking viewers to send money while the people on the screen wear $10,000 watches. Most Christians sincerely believe that the last thing Jesus would wear on His wrist would be a $10,000 watch. And some believe that the second least likely item He would wear on His wrist would be a WWJD bracelet.

This "spiritual statement"—WWJD—has become a fashion fad phenomenon not even Charles Sheldon, author of *In His Steps,* the novel from which the "What would Jesus do?" question came, could have envisioned. Originally, the cloth bracelets were worn to remind the wearer to pause before every major decision or potentially important reaction and simply employ Jesus' criteria to the situation. "Will my actions glorify the Father?" "Will what I'm about to do harm anyone?" "If I do this, will I be building the Kingdom and winning the lost for Christ?" Soon, however, the WWJD logo became less of a moral barometer and more of a fashion statement. The bracelets became silver and gold, then began to be worn as necklaces and rings, and finally made it to the backs of cars and trucks in the form of bumper stickers. And some of those were on BMWs and SUVs!

The Bottom Line

The bottom line of this discussion is literally *the bottom line*. With the fashion industry making as much money as it does, one must wonder where the money goes, and unfortunately, most of it goes to a few at the top. The garment industry has been under scrutiny for years, especially in regard to so-called sweatshops, where employees work 12 to 18 hours a day, seven days a week for about $2 a day (www.greenleft.org.au).

"My salary doesn't help me with anything," says 23-year-old Ruth Meza-Orozco, who has worked six days a week in a clothing factory in Managua, Nicaragua, for the past five years. "I don't even have a house," she says (www.iht.com).

Jesus would find those conditions intolerable. Based on this fact alone, He would probably choose to boycott any item of clothing made under such dire circumstances. Moreover, He would undoubtedly seek to help the Ruth Meza-Orozcos of the world by seeking fair wages and comfortable working conditions for her and all people like her. Much of His work would be on His favorite level, one-on-one, for sure, but it seems as likely that He would also talk to those in charge of sweatshops and the garment industry, imploring them to show compassion and justice to the lowliest of the lowly.

If Jesus were living among us today, He would probably dress as humbly as He dressed 2,000 years ago. Chances are that He would wear a simple cotton shirt, maybe even a T-shirt; inexpensive, practical pants, perhaps blue jeans; and a pair of old, comfortable shoes that hadn't taken money out of Ruth Meza-Orozco's pocket and put it in the wallet of Nike's CEO. He would never wear anything that caused a brother or sister to be abused in its manufacture, nor would He wear anything that brought attention to itself because of its trendy label. If He went shopping with $300 tucked in His pocket and found that a $10 jacket from the thrift store kept Him as warm as a $300 jacket from Banana Republic or Abercrombie & Fitch, He'd opt for the cheaper coat. And then He'd buy 29 more of them for His brothers and sisters at the rescue mission. And one more thing we can count on: Jesus would wear His clothes until they wore out rather than the day some fashion designer informed Him they had gone out of style. Can you imagine?

After all, it was Jesus who told us, "Do not worry about . . . what you will wear. Is not life more important than . . . clothes? . . . See how the lilies of the field grow. . . . Not even Solomon in all his splendor was dressed like one of these. . . . Will he not much more clothe you?" (Matt. 6:25-30).

5—whom would Jesus follow?

A Christian Response to Leadership and Followership

The Scripture

When Jesus saw the crowd around him, he gave orders to cross to the other side of the lake. Then a teacher of the law came to him and said, "Teacher, I will follow you wherever you go."

Jesus replied, "Foxes have holes and birds of the air have nests, but the Son of Man has no place to lay his head."

Another disciple said to him, "Lord, first let me go and bury my father."

But Jesus told him, "Follow me, and let the dead bury their own dead."

Then he got into the boat and his disciples followed him. Without warning, a furious storm came up on the lake, so that the waves swept over the boat. But Jesus was sleeping. The disciples went and woke him, saying, "Lord, save us! We're going to drown!"

He replied, "You of little faith, why are you so afraid?" Then he got up and rebuked the winds and the waves, and it was completely calm.

The men were amazed and asked, "What kind of man is this? Even the winds and the waves obey him!" . . .

As Jesus went on from there, he saw a man named Matthew sitting at the tax collector's booth. "Follow me," he told him, and Matthew got up and followed him.

While Jesus was having dinner at Matthew's house, many tax collectors and "sinners" came and ate with him and his disciples. When the Pharisees saw this, they asked his disciples, "Why does your teacher eat with tax collectors and 'sinners'?"

On hearing this, Jesus said, "It is not the healthy who need a doctor, but the sick. But go and learn what this means: 'I desire mercy, not sacrifice.' For I have not come to call the righteous, but sinners" (Matt. 8:18-27; 9:9-13).

The Discussion

In a world constantly in search of effective leaders, what is needed most today are effective followers.

Every spring, commencement exercises across the nation are full of claims that "this is the next generation of great leaders." What some speaker needs to stand up and say before thousands of graduates and parents is, "This is the next generation of great followers." Parents are equally guilty of downplaying the follower role. Have you ever heard a mother brag to another mother, "My Mary Beth is such a wonderful follower"? There are leadership conferences all over this country every year, but have you ever attended a national *followership* conference? Does that word even exist?

Jesus himself said, "I am among you as one who serves" (Luke 22:27). At that moment, He made being a follower superior to being a leader. What He was saying in essence was, "I have come not to be an effective leader but rather to be a strong follower." It was in His unique ability to follow that He did, indeed, become a great leader. When He said, "The last will be first, and the first will be last" (Matt. 20:16), He was acknowledging that effective followers will become worthy leaders and worthy leaders must also be effective followers.

Good followers are risk-takers because they have discovered methods of dealing with negativity. To a follower, *failure is the salt that flavors success.* In my field, college instruction, a 4.0 grade point average is seen as the ultimate academic goal. It's a tangible symbol of mental acuity and physical perseverance that says to the world, "I came, I saw, I conquered." Most students aspire to the perfect grade point average, but few actually attain it, and that's what makes it so valuable. Can you imagine how fast the prestige of a 4.0 would plummet if every student had one?

Unfortunately, at least it's unfortunate from the students' point of view, I have personally "ruined" many a college experience by "giving" a student his or her "first" or "only" B in his or her entire life, "and I'm gonna lose my scholarship and my parents are gonna kill me and I'm never gonna get into med school." I've always found it intriguing that students *earn* their high grades but teachers *give* them their low grades. I have a wholly different perspective on grades, however, because I've been on both sides of the report card, and as a student, I felt both the elation of a 4.0 (for one quarter of college) and the deflation of failing a college course.

In the first quarter of my junior year, my adviser enrolled me in a senior level political science course in order to fulfill some general education requirement. I was an English major who had no business taking constitutional law from Dr. Woodward, but there I was with all the future lawyers of the Northwest, trying to stay on top of torts and precedents and who knows what else. Four weeks before the term ended, Dr. Woodward gave us our only grade of the semester: the midterm exam. On top was sitting a letter I had never seen in all my life—a big, fat, red F. I thought the world was going to end.

The very next quarter, I worked harder than I had ever worked in school and managed to earn what was for me the pinnacle of achievements, the only 4.0 report card of my entire life. Of course, I spent the entire spring break that followed in hospitals, trying to figure out why I was throwing up blood, but it all seemed worth it.

I think I learned a valuable lesson. No, it wasn't that people should avoid hard work, and it wasn't how a failing student goes about dropping a course in the registrar's office. It wasn't even that hard work brings great rewards. The lesson I learned is that I would never have been able to fully appreciate the flavor of success had I never tasted failure. Effective followers learn that lesson early.

The corollary to this idea is that one is wise to deflect praise and reflect on criticism. Neither should be taken too seriously: absorbing praise creates an egomaniac, and soaking up criticism creates a moody martyr.

Another secret to becoming a good follower is *originality, the ability to transform the same old thing into something brand-new.* I have a twin brother who, for all practical purposes, was my alternate being, my alter ego, as we were growing up. We looked so much alike that when my parents dressed us alike, no one outside the immediate family could tell us apart. Now one of the true benefits of being a twin is that no matter how homely you are, because there are two homely yous, you're automatically called cute. It was only after we split up after college that I realized that I'm not a very handsome man.

It's because of growing up with this sameness that I today have difficulty with mindless repetition or meaningless tradition. I don't want anything to be like I did it the last time, so even thank-you notes become full evenings of designing and writing original cards to everyone on the list. It's so much more work, but it's the only way I can get through the tedium. I have difficulty teaching courses the same way from semester to semester; I always want to keep it fresh so I remain interested. Hey, if the teacher gets bored, the course is doomed before it begins.

One student made a paper airplane in class one day that was so original, I asked him to teach me how to make it. It was a floating cylinder rather than a winged dart, and it flew better than any paper airplane I had ever seen. Another student turned in a book review of a Dickens novel several years ago in the form of a dialogue/interview between two of the main characters. One group of students passed out plastic pearls and string for the entire class to make necklaces last year while discussing John Steinbeck's novel *The Pearl*. Some other person staged a shooting (using a starter's pistol full of blanks) in a photojournalism class I was teaching to show how a good cameraperson is always prepared to document the event on film.

A third characteristic of following is learning how to *lean on others, lean on God, but lean not on one's own understanding alone.* The writer of Proverbs writes (my paraphrase): "Trust in the Lord with all your heart, and don't rely on your own insight. In all your decisions consult him, and he will make your choices seem clear" (3:5). Followers are as capable and talented being delegated to as leaders are capable and talented in delegating. It's the personal recognition of limitations, admitting that "while I may be able to do one thing at a time fairly well, I can't do everything well. I need help."

One of the great blessings of teaching is to watch how students lead groups of their peers, one of the hardest endeavors for any person. Some do it well while most fail miserably. The students who see their groups excel are those who recognize the advantage of delegating the workload. Nowhere is this more evident than on the student newspaper, where student editors are in charge of publishing a weekly chronicle of and commentary on campus events. Editors who thrive in the role have staffs who do most of the work, but editors who have difficulty even surviving the week invariably attempt to do it all themselves.

Even Jesus saw that His mission would be successful only if He delegated the work to a group of 12 loyal brothers. Today, pastors discover—some the hard way—that the model of Christ is the most effective model there is to building a church: delegate and get out of the way.

Fourth, the effective follower is invariably a natural listener. *Listening is respecting; listening is affirming; listening is dignifying; listening is learning.* I doubt I'm the only one who has ever pretended to be listening to someone, then been caught. Like the time a person was in my office, spilling her guts about something that was tearing her life apart, and I chimed in, "Hey, did you happen to catch *Seinfeld* last night?" Or the time one of my freshman classes was reading an essay aloud about the various types of students in a typical college classroom; the moment we began to read the rather derisive description of "The Window Watcher," a student on the third row exclaimed, "Hey, it's snowing outside!" Finally, we all know the horrible feeling of talking to someone who refuses to put down the newspaper or turn down the sound on the television.

Marriage counselors claim that most problems in a relationship start at the failure to turn one's full attention to the other person and truly engage in what he or she is saying. Failing to listen tells the other person that he or she is less important than you are, and that alone makes for very short and shallow relationships. Only when we listen can we learn; no one ever learned anything by speaking.

The gift of listening is enhanced by carving out time each day to listen to ourselves, what I call, "taking a mini-retreat." Whether it's a bike ride or a walk, a lunch alone, or few moments staring out the window, these miniretreats can recharge and reinvigorate one's creative juices enough to make the art of listening more accessible and much more effective.

Michele McCormick, owner of a small public relations firm in California, wrote an essay titled "We're Too Busy for Ideas," published in *Newsweek* (March 29, 1993). In the essay, she reveals how she became so "plugged in" to today's technology that "things stopped occurring to me." She got so caught up in the banality of her Walkman, for instance, that her once growing list of ideas began to shrink. She began to realize that "time spent lost in thought isn't really lost at all. That's why 'unplugged time' is vital. That's when new directions, different approaches and exciting solutions emerge from a place that can't be tapped at will. Creativity comes when we allow our minds to wander freely."

A fifth trait of successful followership is *obedience, the stance of humility and meekness.* Notice that I said meekness, not weakness. Learning how to take an order or follow through with a plan is never a sign of weakness. Jesus taught us that by promising that the "meek . . . will inherit the earth" (Matt. 5:5). He taught us by example when He acquiesced His own will to the will of His Heavenly Father in the garden: "My Father, if it is possible, may this cup be taken from me. Yet not as I will, but as you will" (26:39).

Most of us have suffered the tyranny of an irksome employer, a terrible boss. At the core of the difficulty, most likely, was the inability or unwillingness of the boss to put his or her feet into the boots of the employee. Awful employers were most likely, themselves, awful employees. Ineffective leaders stand behind and *push* their followers rather than forge on ahead and *pull* them toward the goal. Conversely, the mark of a good employee is to do his or her job even before he or she is asked to do it. It's showing initiative and personal integrity of a job not only well done but eagerly done as well.

Finally, following is marked by a *willingness to do whatever it takes to reach the goal.* No task is too small, too trivial; no position is too low, too humiliating; no person is disposable and no possession is indisposable.

When I became a college professor, it marked the culmination of 22 consecutive years of formal education and a lot of money and hard work. So I took great pride that first year in my ivory tower office, overlooking the central courtyard of the campus. I had made the Big Time. Or so I thought.

Then one day, I noticed a transient in an old tweed coat and baggy pants on campus, a burlap sack in one hand and a poker stick in the other, sauntering around the grounds, poking trash and placing it in his sack. I felt sorry for him, but I secretly thanked the Lord that I no longer had to pick up trash for a living—one of my many menial jobs while I was a student.

About a week later, I saw the same old man in the same clothes with the same tools doing the same thing I had witnessed the week before. This went on for several weeks until my curiosity got the better of me. I asked a colleague who had been around much longer than I, "Who's that guy out there and what's he doing?"

She told me that the "guy" was Dr. Fred Floyd, beloved history professor for 40 years, holder of three doctorates, now retired. He had even had a building named after him.

"Well, why is he out there picking up trash?" I asked, oblivious to any reason anyone would do that sort of dirty work voluntarily.

"Oh, that's just his way of showing the students how much he loves them," she said. And suddenly, I knew how much he loved me too.

The Bottom Line

Failure.
Originality.
Leaning.
Listening.
Obedience.
Willingness.

That's how you spell F-O-L-L-O-W. If anyone wants to become a great leader, he or she must first become a great follower. And then stay one.

6—what would Jesus read?

A Christian Response to Censorship, Literacy, and Passive Media

The Scripture

You then, my son, be strong in the grace that is in Christ Jesus. And the things you have heard me say in the presence of many witnesses entrust to reliable men who will also be qualified to teach others. . . .

God's word is not chained. Therefore I endure everything for the sake of the elect, that they too may obtain the salvation that is in Christ Jesus, with eternal glory.

Here is a trustworthy saying:
If we died with him,
    we will also live with him;
if we endure,
    we will also reign with him.
If we disown him,
    he will also disown us;
if we are faithless,
    he will remain faithful,
    for he cannot disown himself.

Keep reminding them of these things. Warn them before God against quarreling about words; it is of no value, and only ruins those who listen. Do your best to present yourself to God as one approved, a workman who does not need to be ashamed and who correctly handles the word of truth. Avoid godless chatter, because those who indulge in it will become more and more ungodly. Their teaching will spread like gangrene. . . . [The King James Version translates verse 15: *Study to show thyself approved unto God, a workman that needeth not to be ashamed, rightly dividing the word of truth.*]

In a large house there are articles not only of gold and silver, but also of wood and clay; some are for noble purposes and some for ignoble. If a man cleanses himself from the latter, he will be an instrument for noble purposes, made holy, useful to the Master and prepared to do any good work.

Flee the evil desires of youth, and pursue righteousness, faith, love and peace, along with those who call on the Lord out of a pure heart. Don't have anything to do with foolish and stupid arguments, because you know they produce quarrels. And the Lord's servant must not quarrel; instead, he must be kind to everyone, able to teach, not resentful. Those who oppose him he must gently instruct, in the hope that God will grant them repentance leading them to a knowledge of the truth, and that they will come to their senses and escape from the trap of the devil, who has taken them captive to do his will (2 Tim. 2:1-2, 9-17, 20-26).

The Discussion

Literature teachers, librarians, and booksellers want us to read everything we can put our eyes on. Often their motives are sincere—they simply want all of us to fall in love with books like they have. Sometimes, though, they know— and soon make all of us very well aware—that their paychecks are dependent on our so-called *love of literature.*

Most mothers and fathers wish their kids would read more. "Can't we all just sit down with a good book tonight and be really, *really* quiet?" (Is this a mom who loves to read or a mom who can't take the uproar one more second?) Again, the motives for these wishes are as varied and valid as the situations in which they arise, but most parents are acutely aware of the value of learning how to read and how to read well. The fact that it often brings a peaceful serenity into the room is only a wonderful *(wonderful)* byproduct but certainly not its primary purpose. (Oh, really?)

Most Americans today read something every day, whether it's the daily newspaper, messages on the computer, and crawlers along the bottom of television screens, or simply traffic signs along the roadways. But for as many as 90 million Americans, reading is a functional impossibility, according to a 1998 government report, "The State of Literacy in America," released by the National Institute for Literacy. "Out of 191 million adults in the U.S.," the report states, "as many as 44 million cannot read a newspaper or fill out a job application. Another 50 million more cannot read or comprehend above the eighth grade level" (www.wsws.org). The South has been hit the hardest, the study reports; the five highest rates of functional illiteracy are in Mississippi (30 percent of the state's adult population), Louisiana (28 percent), Alabama, Florida, and South Carolina (25 percent). "Miami, Florida, reported 63 percent of its residents at the Level I (functional illiteracy) literacy level" (www.wsws.org).

Unfortunately, in a society dependent on the ability to read, illiteracy translates into unemployment, poverty, homelessness, crime, and in the cases of medical instructions, death. *The Journal of the American Medical Association* reported in 1995 that 75 percent of patients in two urban hospitals studied could not understand a simple medical consent form. Furthermore, according to several other studies, the prison population [now at 2 million] represents the single highest concentration of illiterate U.S. adults (www.wsws.org).

Despite the political promises of several administrations, the primary tool against illiteracy continues to be volunteers. Much of this is due to severe cuts in educational budgets (professional teachers), both on the state and federal levels. Charles Hunter, a spokesperson for the National Institute for Literacy, says, "Our aim is to work with businesses and industry to give them ideas on what they can do. If a company calls us, we will direct them on what they can do. We try to give them ideas besides giving money. There are many little things they can do like allowing an employee to help tutor by volunteering, helping work peers, etc." (www.wsws.org).

Mark Twain once quipped, "The man who does not read books has no advantage over the man who can't read them." For some, then, illiteracy is a choice—"I just don't wanna read." But among those people who can read and then actually *choose* to read, many discover that their choices of what is available to read are being made by other people. This notion of censorship is hottest when it comes to curricular decisions in the public schools of America.

Those on one side claim that children, even children up through high school grades, should not be exposed to certain books or philosophies. On the other side of the issue are those who believe that any kind of censorship represents a direct attack on the United States Constitution and Bill of Rights.

Among the novels most commonly contested in public school libraries are Mark Twain's *The Adventures of Huckleberry Finn, Hamlet* by William Shakespeare, *The Scarlet Letter* by Nathaniel Hawthorne, *I Know Why the Caged Bird Sings* by Maya Angelou, *Catcher in the Rye* by J. D. Salinger, and R. L. Stine's *Goosebumps* series. Some of these are questioned because of their language (inappropriate), and some are challenged because of their themes (racism or sexuality). According to *Education World,* other reasons for censoring a book include the book's references to drugs, children challenging parental authority, evolution, and nontraditional roles for women (www.educationworld.com).

"The urge to censor is hardly the monopoly of any political group," says that bastion of liberalism, the American Civil Liberties Union. "But the greatest *threat* [my italics] today comes from the fundamentalist right, with its ideological hostility to other religious or philosophical systems, . . . and to the basic idea of secular education" (www.rethinkingschools.org). The so-called fundamentalist right defends its motives with its allegiance to wholesome family values and religious morality—both ideals that are difficult to dispute or refute. Don Ernst, director of government relations at the Association for the Supervision of Curriculum and Development, tries to build a bridge between the two hard lines: "The health of a democracy is not so much about how people agree but how they choose to disagree. Students need to have the skills, the abilities to critique and analyze a wide array of viewpoints" (www.rethinkingschools.org).

Once an individual leaves formal schooling, the choices of what to read and what not to read fall directly on his or her shoulders, or heart, if you will. Some are resolved to read only material that agrees with their personal philosophies and/or religious tenets, and there is inherently nothing wrong with that. Others want to read material that is diametrically opposed to their own ideals or personal agendas for any of a number of reasons, whether it is to open their horizons or expand their worldviews. And it would be hard to argue against either presumably noble aspiration.

A final consideration in this issue centers on television, today's most passive yet pervasive medium. Although the number of books being published seems to increase marginally every year, the number of people actually reading them tends to decline. What is happening, then, is that fewer people are reading more books, and conversely, more people are reading fewer books. As will be discussed in the chapter, "What Would Jesus Watch?" the dynamic of information acquisition and retention is far different when television is the messenger than when the more traditional purveyors of information—like books, magazines, and newspapers—are "on." This is not to condemn television viewing, whatsoever; it is to point out, however, that a steady diet of television exclusive of actively participating in the message, as happens in reading, slackens mental acuity and stunts one's knowledge base.

The Bottom Line

There were not very many books available for Jesus to read; the only thing that was even remotely ready was the Talmud (the Jewish law), but only then in the Temple. Jewish writings would have been just about the only "primer" around for children to read at all. That may sound terribly limited to modern-day readers, but we must remember that Christ's culture did not exist in this information age of ours. His was a culture that learned much more by tuning in and turning on to people's hearts and minds than to their e-mail addresses or personal libraries.

It is because of this historical and cultural gap, then, that trying to predict what Jesus would read is really as much a matter of "What would I, as a follower of Jesus, read?" as it is anything close to a definitive reading list. Some writers and scholars are much more comfortable discussing what Jesus *wouldn't* read than what He *would* read. Cathleen Falsani, a religion writer for the *Chicago Sun-Times,* claims with her tongue firmly imbedded in her cheek that Jesus would read anything but the Timothy LaHaye *Left Behind* series because He already knows how it ends (November 22, 2002).

Obviously, His Father's Holy Book, actually a holy library of 66 holy books, would be a constant entry on His Top Ten, but chances are pretty good that if He walked among us today, He would also read books that encourage the human spirit and check human excesses. Some of today's writing He would sincerely appreciate, but most, probably, He would put down with a smile or smirk and say, "Now that was interesting. I wonder how her thinking will change when she joins me in Paradise."

There are lots of theories and programs about how one *should* read the Bible. Some people believe that they must read the entire Scripture, Genesis to Revelation, every year, a goal not without its own sense of nobility. Others believe, on the other hand, that the more productive method is to read one of the 66 books every year. Still others narrow that goal to reading (studying might be the more accurate term) only one chapter of one book every year. Most churches and catechisms teach that one must read from the Bible every day, no matter how many or few verses are read; a lot of us grew up with a great deal of guilt heaped upon our spirits if we failed to read a passage of the Bible every day. The fact of the matter is, there is no prescribed standard or method of properly digesting God's Word. He said in John's account, "You have never heard his voice nor seen his form, nor does his word dwell in you, for you do not believe the one he sent. You diligently study the Scriptures because you think that by them you possess eternal life. These are the Scriptures that testify about me, yet you refuse to come to me to have life" (5:37-40). It's not the reading that gives one eternal life: it's faith and obedience to the Word that open the gates to Paradise.

Jesus would, indeed, keep up with what was happening in the world by reading a newspaper every day, but if the newspaper of His hometown was politically extreme or simply poor quality, He might pick up another newspaper or two down at the local coffeehouse. His life was all about balance, so His news consumption would be balanced as well. His favorite section would certainly be the editorial page with all those intriguing letters to the editor, and He'd presumably respond much like you and I do: an occasional, "That's right!" punctuated with a "Whatever!" once in a while.

Jesus might subscribe to magazines if He felt they enhanced His ministry. That's not to say He would read only religious magazines, but He would probably not look at too many purely leisure magazines about sports or fashion or interior decorating. It's also doubtful He would spend much time with gossip or celebrity magazines.

In fact, Jesus would ostensibly not waste His precious

hours reading most of what one can borrow at the library or buy at the bookstore these days. Any writing that disparaged His Father or trivialized His creation or creations would probably not grab His heartfelt attention, at least not in a positive way. Language that demeaned men and women, dismissing them as beings bent on violence or self-gratification, would be highly offensive to Him. Themes that alienated groups of people from one another, particularly out of hatred or vengeance, would cause Him to turn away.

When one reads about Jesus' life in the four Gospels, one comes away truly believing that He was 100 percent driven to lift people up to places of grace and pure reconciliation. Nothing He did among His disciples, family, or extended spiritual family strayed from that divine mission, and it would be misguided, to say the least, to suggest that He would choose to read today anything counter to that overriding purpose.

Paul reflects that same ideal in his second letter to Timothy. When he comes to that wonderfully rich passage about the large house (vv. 20-21), the reader might do well to read it metaphorically in this current context: "In a large library/ bookstore (house), there are many books (articles) not only of great value (gold and silver), but also of no value whatsoever (wood and clay); some are for noble purposes and some for ignoble. If a man cleanses himself from the latter, he will be an instrument for noble purposes, made holy, useful to the Master and prepared to do any good work."

Of course, now having written this chapter, I have to wonder, would Jesus ever read this book?

7—what would Jesus play?

A Christian Response to Leisure, Recreation, Fitness, and Exercise

The Scripture

Do you not know that your body is a temple of the Holy Spirit, who is in you, whom you have received from God? You are not your own; you were bought at a price. Therefore honor God with your body (1 Cor. 6:19-20).

The Discussion

In the context of this passage from Paul's first letter to the church at Corinth, he is speaking about sexual purity, but the principles applied to that aspect of one's physical habits can be applied equally, it seems, to other activities of the body, such as playing, exercising, and general physical fitness. If our bodies are indeed the houses of God's Spirit, then how we treat them becomes a spiritual issue.

Because we live in a culture that runs on money, Americans have turned even something as rudimentary as playing into a multimillion-dollar enterprise. From the incredibly egregious salaries of professional athletes to the T-ball leagues that dominate our Saturdays, from mammoth fitness centers in every community to spandex biking shorts on every trail, from so-called sports drinks to the current fascination with steroids, sports with a capital S have become more than America's pastime; they've become America's obsession.

Historically, playing games has been around for centuries; the ancient Olympics can be traced to Roman times. Even some of the drawings on cave walls by our earliest ancestors indicate human beings have always played games. It has only been in the last 100 to 150 years, however, that the idea of sports and their entitlements has become so deeply engrained in Americana. When people began working indoors in an industrialized economy, playing outdoors became its logical diversion. As Americans became wealthier, more money for leisurely activities became available, so professional leagues were founded. Not only did this allow us to showcase our most skilled athletes, but it also enabled those who liked sports, along with their hot dogs and Cracker Jacks and 44-ounce Cokes, to sit on the sidelines and watch. No, it wasn't really the kind of exercise that actually benefited the body of the bleacher bum, but it almost felt like it.

When television took over our lives in the mid-20th century, sports on television was sure to follow. The first World Series game was broadcast on October 6, 1947, and soon after, fans were treated to occasional Sunday games of the NFL. By the 1960s, a sports fan could get his or her fill of football and baseball every weekend, and in the 1970s, when live television was made possible through satellites, hockey, boxing, basketball, Olympics, and more athletic events were woven into the American fabric. Fifteen years later, cable television began to grow, and today, one can watch sports 24 hours a day, seven days a week. If there were 25 hours in a day or eight days in a week, we'd watch sports then too.

This phenomenon alone has changed the landscape of sports in our society. Before the glut of sportscasts took over our family rooms, most of us were much more involved with playing games. And that's exactly what they were called: games. When our Saturday chores were finished, we grabbed as many friends as we could find in our urban and suburban neighborhoods, headed over to the local schoolyard with our balls and mitts and bats, and played all afternoon. There were no uniforms, no umpires, no coaches, and most importantly, no scoreboard. That's not to say score was not important—scoring the go-ahead touchdown or hitting the game-winning home run were, indeed, the stuff of sweet dreams at night. But who won or lost yesterday or last week was never the most important thing about playing. No, *playing* was the most important part about playing, and that was something that one could do every day. From scratch, start-overs included.

When did we become so serious about our playtime?

Today, sports for kids, especially, are very, very different. Official leagues have taken over neighborhood choose-'em-ups. Sanctioned batting practice has replaced workups. Summertime sports camps, team sponsors, league schedules and standings are all now parts of every kid's youth. And while most participants are still having barrels of fun, learning the differences between a zone defense and a run-and-gun offense, watching their friends succeed on the diamond or flop on the gridiron, too many kids and adults take all of this very, very seriously.

Part of the reason lies in the money invested in such endeavors. Because hundreds of dollars are now spent on equipment, fees, travel, insurance, and so forth, the difference between winning and losing has become exaggerated. To lose a game, these days, is to lose money on an investment, and as the child progresses through league after league, level after level, the stakes get that much higher.

Sports have also become a means to an end rather than a simple end in themselves. The ability to shoot three-pointers or hit the long ball or run through the line has become one's ticket to *big money*. Poor kids see the inflated salary of their sports hero rather than the rigors of a long and sometimes tedious education as their escape hatch from poverty. And even if education is a priority, getting into the right university is often dependent on earning an athletic scholarship. This suddenly transforms Saturday's *game* into a life-and-death struggle.

Sociologists and psychologists are now studying sports and athletics as they relate to things like suicide, homicide, cheating, plagiarism, and neighborhood violence.

Jesus would undoubtedly have trouble with a lot of this artificial pressure to excel in playing games, to win at all costs, to vanquish our foes, and to annihilate the opposition. Particularly if that excellence and victory come at the cost of loving one another as ourselves, of turning the other cheek to our adversaries, of loving our enemies and laying down our lives for our brothers and sisters. Not to mention the proper Christian stewardship of our time and money.

Much of the discussion to this point may seem like there is nothing but a downside to participating in recreational exercise, but there are actually a significant number of physical benefits to fitness. First and foremost, exercising the body is the most effective method of living a long and healthful life. What we eat, how much we sleep, what bad habits we avoid, and so on are all important factors to consider, to be sure, but without regular and vigorous exercise, none of the rest of it really matters that much. Nutrition goes a long way toward building a sound and robust lifestyle, but no diet alone can bring the level of health required for longevity. On the other hand, eating all the wrong things cannot be overcome simply by picking up the barbell or accelerating the heart rate. One must aim for proper balance.

Exercise makes the heart healthy. "What we've been doing for quite some time is determining the beneficial effects of exercise on lipids," says Stephen Crouse, an associate professor in health and kinesiology at Texas A&M University, who is studying the relationship between exercise and the health of the human heart. "We have found that we can effectively produce changes in lipids with a single bout of exercise," he said. "Exercise tends to improve the cholesterol status of the blood—raising the level of good cholesterol, or HDL, and lowering the bad, or LDL." The risk of heart attack and stroke increases in direct proportion to increases of LDL. "If exercise will work as an effective prevention, the patient may not need to spend money on medication," he said (*AggieDaily,* 12/5/96, www.tamu.edu).

How much exercise is needed to retain an overall sense of health? The National Academies' Institute of Medicine, the institute that congress refers to when it comes to health legislation, advised in 2002 that at least 60 minutes of moderate exercise a day is needed to regulate weight and retain a healthy heart. For those who can't imagine spending that much time exercising every day, one former surgeon general of the United States said in 1996 that 30 minutes a day, five days a week would do the trick. Others have said, "Anything is better than nothing" (www.active.com). What are we to believe?

It helps to differentiate the terms "physical activity" and "physical exercise." According to active.com, the former simply "breaks a sweat," while the latter "pushes to a point just shy of breathlessness." But this 60 minutes doesn't have to be all at once; one might find it easier to break up the time into two, three, or even six smaller increments. Doctors recommend some easy ways to achieve this. Park as far from the door of your destination as you can and walk. Whenever possible, take the stairs rather than the elevator or escalator. Crank the ice-cream maker rather than plug in the electric motor. Push the edger instead of using a gas- or electric-powered machine. Ride a bike on errands rather than driving a car. Even gardening is healthy exercise. "Studies show that briskly walking 30 minutes a day can lower the risk of heart disease by 30 to 40 percent" (www.active.com).

Many people couldn't fit another minute of anything into their tight schedules, much less 60 minutes of near breathlessness, which kind of sounds unpleasant, if you want to know the truth. Workaholics tend to be some of the guiltiest people when it comes to the idea of making time to exercise. This is where the freedom of choice comes into play. When we say, "I don't have time" for this or that, what we're really admitting is, "I won't make time" for it; in other words, "That's just not a high priority for me." If it *were* a high priority, we would certainly carve out enough time in our schedules to do it. After all, we've carved out time slots all day for those activities we have deemed *high priority.* The question really becomes, then, "At what point am I going to make my health a high priority?"

It's not just lazy people who don't exercise enough; it's busy people too. That's why achieving this sense of balance in our lives is so important. Working 18-hour days or six-day weeks is every bit as unhealthy as lying on the couch and watching television seven hours every night of the week. One must build into his or her schedule some down-time as well as some exercise time.

And if schedules and appointments and agendas and regimens are not your thing, then maybe simply changing one little thing, like walking to church or biking to the store, will be your initiation into this idea of exercise and fitness.

Most of us know someone who belongs to a health club, a phrase that almost borders on *oxymoronism.* Nothing wrong with belonging to a health club, particularly if one actually uses it to improve his or her physical health. But a lot of people don't have another $40 or $50 a month to shell out for such a club, so here's a bit of advice for them. Rather than driving three or four miles to the club in order to climb aboard a treadmill for an hour or two, simply walk those three or four miles to the front door of the club, turn around, and walk home. You'll get an equal workout without spending all the dough.

The Bottom Line

"Fitness reduces your risk of death. It doesn't get much more *bottom line* than that" (www.active.com).

Jesus was fit. He ate healthfully and in moderation. He walked just about everywhere He went. He got away from His work when He needed to (note how many chapters in the Gospels start or end with "and Jesus went to the other side of the lake"), and made time to do what He deemed important. He did not join a ball team or bowling league or fitness center in order to stay healthy; He didn't need to. Fitness was built into the way He lived.

Most of us don't have that sort of natural fitness because that lifestyle is nearly impossible in our culture. Therefore, we have to find other ways to stay healthy. Too many of us walk every day about as much as Jesus drove, so we have to *make* ourselves walk when we get home or before we come to work in order to burn all the calories we eat at McDonald's for lunch. (You don't want to know this, but you really need to walk at least five miles to burn off a typical fast-food lunch. And that's walking as fast as you can.)

Fitness is not simply related to exercise. We also need to work less and play more. We need to sleep more, too. The latest findings show that half of the drivers on the road, those people you pass every day on your way to and from work, are sleep deprived. That means half the people you drive past today didn't get enough sleep last night—maybe you're one of them. Sleep deprivation has the same effect on one's ability to drive as excessive blood-alcohol levels; therefore, if a person drives unrested, he or she is figuratively driving under the influence. That is a frightening revelation.

Finally, allowing our bodies, the temples of the Holy Spirit, to fall into disrepair profoundly affects our witness to the world. As much as we try to avoid some vices like smoking, drinking, and excessive eating in order to enhance our health and maintain the Holy Spirit's dwelling, we should also endeavor to stay fit.

Jesus did.

8—what would Jesus watch?

A Christian Response to Movies, Television, and Advertising

The Scripture

Then some Pharisees and teachers of the law came to Jesus from Jerusalem and asked, "Why do your disciples break the tradition of the elders? They don't wash their hands before they eat!"

Jesus replied, "And why do you break the command of God for the sake of your tradition? For God said, 'Honor your father and mother' and 'Anyone who curses his father or mother must be put to death.' But you say that if a man says to his father or mother, 'Whatever help you might otherwise have received from me is a gift devoted to God,' he is not to 'honor his father' with it. Thus you nullify the word of God for the sake of your tradition. You hypocrites! Isaiah was right when he prophesied about you:

"'These people honor me with their lips,
    but their hearts are far from me.
They worship me in vain;
    their teachings are but rules taught by men.'"

Jesus called the crowd to him and said, "Listen and understand. What goes into a man's mouth does not make him 'unclean,' but what comes out of his mouth, that is what makes him 'unclean.'"

Then the disciples came to him and asked, "Do you know that the Pharisees were offended when they heard this?"

He replied, "Every plant that my heavenly Father has not planted will be pulled up by the roots. Leave them; they are blind guides. If a blind man leads a blind man, both will fall into a pit."

Peter said, "Explain the parable to us."

"Are you still so dull?" Jesus asked them. "Don't you see that whatever enters the mouth goes into the stomach and then out of the body? But the things that come out of the mouth come from the heart, and these make a man 'unclean.' For out of the heart come evil thoughts, murder, adultery, sexual immorality, theft, false testimony, slander. These are what make a man 'unclean'; but eating with unwashed hands does not make him 'unclean'" (Matt. 15:1-20).

The Discussion

Obviously, Jesus didn't go to movies. Neither did He sit all evening on His couch, remote in one hand and a root beer float in the other, feet propped up and mind sitting comfortably in neutral, scanning through police dramas, dysfunctional family sitcoms, or worse: reality TV. He was not lured by hundreds of colorful and provocative advertisements every day that attempted to sell Him things He would never really need and certainly never want.

Jesus and His disciples, even the Pharisees themselves, were speaking here about a consumption characterized more by food and drink than by anything cinematic. But the principles applied in Matthew's passage might be aptly applied to this discussion as well: it's what comes out rather than what goes in that defiles. This is the reasoning, after all, denominations have heard and employed over the years as the debate rages on about whether or not Christians should attend the theater. The side that has wanted to go to movies has claimed that they are wise, mature, and discerning enough to remain untainted by the movies they watch; the side that has wanted to keep church members out of the theater has stated that the influence of the silver screen casts a mighty dark shadow over the wooden Cross.

This idea might, quite frankly, leave the ethical door far

too wide open for most people because if applied literally and universally, it suggests a rather hedonistic, anything-goes attitude. One might proclaim nothing off limits—no movie inappropriate, no television program unsuitable, no advertisement offensive—as long as one is able to prevent those stimuli from surfacing in his or her behavior or thought-life. "As long as what comes out of my mouth [and mind] is not defiling me or others, it doesn't really matter what goes in my mouth [and mind]."

Unfortunately, there are few people in the world who can proclaim with any credibility that they are not greatly influenced by what they put into their minds. Human beings are simply not capable of remaining unaffected by what they read, watch, see, or hear; in fact, the synergy of our minds and bodies is wired to do just the opposite. We are genetically programmed to alter our behavior when we discover through our sensory organs the benefits or drawbacks of certain behaviors. When we burn our fingers on the stove, we learn that oven mitts or extinguished flames make our lives more painless; conversely, we learn that forgetting to put on the mitt or turn off the burner will bring us more pain. When parents discipline their children for disobeying, children's minds remember the consequences they suffer so that next time their decisions will be better aligned to parents' expectations. When we taste offensive food, we don't eat it again; when we bang our fingers with a hammer because we forgot to put on our glasses, we make sure we're wearing our glasses next time something needs hammering; when we walk across rocky ground, we wear our shoes.

In his book *The Principles of Jesus,* Robert Speer suggests that when Jesus was explaining the parable of the sower and said, "The seed that fell among the thorns stands for those who hear, but as they go on their way they are choked by life's worries, riches and pleasures, and they do not mature," he was referring to "frivolous, light-minded, superficial things . . . that merely please the senses or give little passing physical pleasure, or serve to kill time—the theater, cards, dancing, eating for the sake of eating, dress" (214).

But Speer immediately dispels the idea that Jesus condemned all pleasures in life. "He went to a marriage feast with His disciples (John 2:1, 2). He told His disciples what to do when they made feasts (Luke 14:13); and He accepted invitations to other social festivities (Luke 5:29; John 12:2; Matt. 9:11; Luke 13:26). Indeed, this was so regularly His custom that, criticizing His associations, the Pharisees called Him 'a gluttonous man and a wine bibber'" (Luke 5:30; 7:34) (215). In the Pharisaic world of rules, Jesus broke far too many to be accepted—can you imagine? Speer concludes that Jesus attended such things exclusively as "occasions for spiritual teaching (Luke 7:36-50; 11:37-40; 14:1-14). He sought no physical indulgence," and "did not seek or desire worldly pleasure"; "as an end in itself He could never have approved it" (215).

Could Jesus have been reflecting His Father's future disapproval of movies when He taught in the Great Sermon, "Do not store up for yourselves treasures on earth, where moth and rust destroy, and where thieves break in and steal. But store up for yourselves treasures in heaven, where moth and rust do not destroy, and where thieves do not break in and steal" (Matt. 6:19-20)? Of course, we can't know for certain the answer since movies were not a part of Jesus' culture, but certainly these principles of Christ can be applied to theater and television.

It seems easy to say that Jesus would be far too busy in today's society to sit in front of a television set for several hours a night, and far too careful in His stewardship to plop down $10 to attend a movie (and another $10 for popcorn and a Coke). But then, it could also be said that He would be too involved in the seriousness and importance of building His Father's kingdom to spend precious hours reading a good suspense novel or attending an invigorating Broadway play or even training for and running in the Boston Marathon. Unless He would see all those things as merely means to His eternal ends. Speer says, "Jesus came to lift the whole set of life's tastes and desires to a new and higher plane of pleasure, to fill men with joy; but the joy not of sense, but of spirit, not of this world only, but of the world to come as well" (217).

It seems, then, a valid question to ask, "What ends would justify watching television or attending the theater?" In her book *Mind and Media,* Patricia Marks Greenfield says, "Television and film can . . . be used to enhance the comprehension and enjoyment of literature. Some teachers are beginning to take advantage of television's ability to motivate reading. A survey of sixth, seventh, and eighth graders in New Jersey showed that 40 percent of the books they chose to read were tied to television or movies. Greenfield cites a story by Rosemary Lee Potter, a "pioneer in the use of out-of-school television in school" (135).

One day a sixth grader named Clara came in with a paperback copy of *Little House on the Prairie.* Clara was not a great reader. I had never seen her with an unassigned book. It was quite a surprise for me to see her bring in a rather thickish book and read it. No doubt noticing my surprise, she quickly explained to me that *she had seen it on TV!* . . . I scoured bookshelves, libraries, and booklists . . . I found a bounty of television-related books for my students . . . I began to bring these books into the classroom. Students showed high interest. Most of the books soon fell apart with excessive wear" (quoted by Greenfield, 135-36).

Perhaps, then, motivating students to read would be an end that justifies the means. And as a result of the reading, teaching becomes an end that would justify the means. Could Jesus have motivated and taught, using what He and the crowds had seen on television the night before or in the theater last weekend? Of course. He frequently used the everyday occurrences in life as tools for His life-changing lessons.

Dorothy Rabinowitz, writing for *The Washington Times,* says, "Study after study shows that school children today come better prepared to learn, and more informed, as a result of television, than any generation before" (quoted by Greenfield, 136). And what was true in 1987 is even truer today with the introduction of personal computers and the Internet. Would Jesus have owned a personal computer and written e-mails and surfed the World Wide Web? As a means to His ends, yes. Obviously, media have raised the level of expertise and expedited the world of communication.

Others have been quite critical of television's influence, especially on children. It would be naive, if not misleading, for anyone to suggest that movies and television have not also brought about huge changes in family and societal dynamics. Programs like "The Simpsons" and "Family Ties" in the 1980s were among the first of many programs to follow that have upturned the hierarchy of the home, showing children as the authorities and parents as the buffoons. Anyone who watches these shows can readily discern that Alex P. Keaton of "Family Ties," played by Michael J. Fox, was the leader of that home, and that Bart Simpson merely tolerates the slapstick ineptitude of his father, Homer, in each of those episodes.

Second, violence on television and in movies has desensitized most of American culture to the tragic consequences of murder, assault, rape, and burglary. The rise in mass murders, particularly among the young, has been allegedly linked by media critics to the glut of violent behavior on both the small and large screen. There seems to be a great shift in the ethics of doing wrong among today's youth: "If I don't get caught, then I didn't do anything wrong," which is manifested, among other things, in the rise in sales of radar detectors for drivers who want to break speed limit laws without getting caught. (Parents who place these devices on their dashboards are teaching their children by example that the secret to being a "law-abiding, upstanding, moral citizen" is simply doing what you want as long as you don't get caught.)

Third, advertising on television, as well as on billboards and in magazines, has raised a generation of girls, particularly, who suffer from life-threatening eating disorders. The pursuit of the ideal body as portrayed by models and actresses, a body that is anatomically impossible to achieve naturally, by the way, has driven thousands of young women into the clutches of starvation, bingeing, and purging. Most of these victims become too sick to function and too weak to remain in school or their jobs. Many die.

Neil Postman, in an essay published in the book *The Mass Media—Opposing Viewpoints,* says, "Television offers . . . three commandments that form the philosophy of the education which television offers: 'Thou shalt have no prerequisites'; 'Thou shalt induce no perplexity'; 'Thou shalt avoid exposition like the ten plagues visited upon Egypt'" (142-43). In other words, television teaches with no necessity of knowing what happened before or after. Each lesson, each program is self-packaged. There is no chronology, no hierarchy, no historical relationship between events or characters. In the world of television "there must be nothing that has to be remembered, studied, applied or, worst of all, endured," Postman concludes (143). He goes on to say that "arguments, hypotheses, discussions, reasons, refutations, or any of the traditional instruments of reasoned discourse turn television into radio, or, worse, third-rate printed matter" (143).

The Bottom Line

So, in the end, would Jesus watch movies, television, and advertising? And if He would, what would He watch and what would He turn off and away from? He would watch those programs or movies that edified and lifted the human spirit. He would watch those presentations that brought Him into a closer spiritual relationship with His Heavenly Father and His next-door neighbor, coworker, best friend. He would watch those things that were viable and irreplaceable means to His ends of building the kingdom of God and ushering us all through its gates for eternal communion with Him. He would shun any movie or television program or advertisement that glorified violence, sexual exploitation, or self-gratification; valorized war or vilified people; promoted greed or individual power over other individuals; or revoked any biblical truth.

9—when would Jesus laugh?

A Christian Response to the Psychological and Physiological Benefits of Humor

The Scripture

Shout for joy to the LORD, all the earth. Worship the LORD with gladness; come before him with joyful songs.

Know that the LORD is God. It is he who made us, and we are his; we are his people, and the sheep of his pasture.

Enter his gates with thanksgiving and his courts with praise; give thanks to him and praise his name.

For the LORD is good and his love endures forever; his faithfulness continues through all generations (Ps. 100).

The Discussion

Frankly, the Bible is pretty quiet when it comes to the idea of laughter, and when it does bring it up, it's awfully negative about it.

"Even in laughter the heart may ache, and joy may end in grief" (Prov. 14:13).

"'Laughter,' I said, 'is foolish. And what does pleasure accomplish?'" (Eccles. 2:2).

"There is a time for everything, and a season for every activity under heaven: . . . a time to weep and a time to laugh, a time to mourn and a time to dance" (3:1, 4).

"Sorrow is better than laughter, because a sad face is good for the heart. The heart of the wise is in the house of mourning, but the heart of fools is in the house of pleasure. It is better to heed a wise man's rebuke than to listen to the song of fools. Like the crackling of thorns under the pot, so is the laughter of fools. This too is meaningless" (7:3-6).

Even James's letter in the New Testament gives laughter a bad rap: "Grieve, mourn and wail. Change your laughter to mourning and your joy to gloom" (4:9).

Luke's recording of Jesus' great sermon on the hillside gives a more hopeful aspect to laughter in the third beatitude: "Blessed are you who weep now, for you will laugh" (6:21), but follows it up with this ominous warning: "Woe to you who laugh now, for you will mourn and weep" (v. 25).

There are many Christians who truly believe Jesus never laughed; after all, given the state of the world at the time, what would He have found so funny? And have things gotten all that much better or lighter-hearted since He ascended to heaven 2,000 years ago? The Gospels record that He *wept* (John 11:35), that He got *angry* (Matt. 12:34; 21:12-16), and that He got *frustrated* (Matt. 22:29; 26:42; Mark 4:40; Luke 2:49), but not once is it said, "And Jesus wrapped His arms around His own belly and heaved a giant hee-haw."

Even so, why would He not have displayed the full spectrum of human emotions; why is it difficult for us to imagine that once in a while He let out a sincere hoot, a chuckle, a giggle, a guffaw? Don't you think He might have at least smiled when James and John were arguing about which of the Twelve was the greatest? Wouldn't He have been happy enough to grin when the paralyzed man got up and danced? Could He not have enjoyed the remark of the guest at the wedding, when He noted that the "good wine" was saved for last?

If Jesus felt as highly about the human spirit as He says He did, then He would at least have appreciated the benefits of laughter. "Laughter increases muscular and respiratory activity. It stimulates the cardiovascular system, the sympathetic nervous system, and the production of catecholamines (neurotransmitters and hormones). It increases antibodies—the body's first line of defense against respiratory illness. It decreases levels of stress hormones. It decreases heart rate (in 'heavy laughers'). It increases pain tolerance. It stimulates the muscular and skeletal systems" (Shara Rendell-Smock, *Humour and Health*, "A Matter of Perspective," Part 3, Issue 11, Jan. 13, 1998, www.sideroad.com). Rendell-Smock concludes that "humor changes our feelings, thoughts, behaviors, and biochemistry. It's all in our perspective. We can develop and nurture humor to heal."

Dr. Lee Berk and Dr. Stanley Tan from Loma Linda University in California found in their 2002 study of the relationship between laughter and the human immune system, "an increase in the number and activity level of natural killer cells that attack viral infected cells and some types of cancer and tumor cells . . . laughter appears to tell the immune system to 'turn it up a notch.'" Laughter also seems to decrease the stress hormones "that constrict blood vessels and suppress immune activity" ("Therapeutic Benefits of Laughter," 2002, www.holistic-online.com).

As a person laughs, several *good things* begin to happen. Muscles all over the body begin to relax whereas those muscles on the face constrict, thereby exercising away potential wrinkles. Oxygen intake increases and, therefore, more carbon dioxide is driven out of the body's system. "It can produce anti-inflammatory agents which can aid back pain or arthritis, [and] it boosts the production of 'feel-good' endorphin hormones," according to an article published in the *Wall Street Journal* (Sumit Sharma, "Stressed? Inhibited? Grumpy? Join the (Laughing) Club, Indian Says," December 9, 1996).

Norman Cousins, an American journalist who was suffering from an incurable disease of the spine, was benefited by laughter therapy when no painkiller could help him. Endorphins released as a result of laughter may help in reducing the intensity of pain in those suffering from arthritis, spondylitis, and muscular spasms of the body. Many women have reported a reduced frequency of migraine headaches ("Health Benefits of Laughter Therapy," www.laughteryoga.org).

Dr. Steven M. Sultanoff, mirthologist and clinical psychologist from Irvine, California, questions a lot of this *data,* however. He calls such findings, "humor legends." He does admit, though, that "laughter clearly affects our physiology. We know heart rate increases, blood flow increases, muscles convulse, and probably hundreds of biochemical changes occur. What's not clear is the exact nature of the biochemical changes." He concludes that "humor is emotionally, cognitively, and biochemically healing, but I am also aware that the research to support my belief is insufficient" ("Examining the Research in the Therapeutic Benefits of Humor and Laughter," 1999, www.humormatters.com).

In one study reported in the *Mind/Body Health Newsletter* (Vol. 8, No. 2, 1999) and cited by Sultanoff, researchers found that among the 12 participating patients, "heart attack survivors who experience 30 minutes of humor daily are less likely to experience second heart attacks, required lower doses of medication, and had lower blood pressure" (www.humormatters.com).

Not only do most scientists agree to the physiological benefits of laughter, but they also raise some of the psychological advantages to laughing every day. "Laughter brings people together and improves interpersonal relationships," according to *Laughter Club International.* "When you are laughing in a group at a public place with your arms up towards the sky, it removes your inhibitions and over a period of time you become a more sociable, unreserved, and outgoing person. Gradually, it adds to your self confidence, personality and leadership qualities," the *LCI* goes on to claim (www.laughteryoga.org).

Hospitals around the country are using laughter as healing therapy. Not only does laughter seem to help the patient deal with his or her pain, sometimes relieving it altogether, but the long-term positive effects of daily laughter

in combating the diseases and injuries, directly, are beginning to pile up. The comedian/actor Robin Williams portrayed one of these *mirthologists* in the 1999 film *Patch
Adams,* based on the real life of the doctor and clown by
that name. Dr. Adams is also a social activist who has spent
the last 30 years attempting to change America's "expensive and elitist" healthcare system (www.bullfrogfilms.com).

Jesus apparently used His *other* gifts and talents when
He sought to heal someone's body or spirit. He cast out
demons, made mud packs, and befriended loners. He fed
hungry people, ate with sinners, and rescued condemned
prisoners. But the Word of God is also clear that the kingdom of God has many members, each with a different gift.
"In the church God has appointed first of all apostles, second prophets, third teachers, then workers of miracles, also
those having gifts of healing, those able to help others,
those with gifts of administration, and those speaking in
different kinds of tongues" (1 Cor. 12:28-30). It is not our
place to suggest that the gift of healing cannot manifest itself alongside the gift of making people laugh, is it?

Jesus would never laugh, however, at the expense of an
individual's self-image or even of the image of a group of
people. Therefore, "jokes" that are racial, ethnic, about other nationalities might, indeed, offend Him. It's hard to
imagine, after all, the Son of the Creator of All Things using
any human being, His ultimate creation, as a prop or punch
line.

This sounds awfully "high and mighty," doesn't it? Almost pious? To suggest that an occasional "blonde joke" or
"political slam" or "denominational jab" offends the ears of
the Almighty makes it seem like we serve a Father-God
completely devoid of all humor. After all, if we can't poke
fun at ourselves and each other, who's left? Won't we all
begin to take ourselves a little too seriously?

All valid questions. The line between *humor* and *offense*
is a fine line, indeed, straddled by many a late-night come-

dian. The secret lies in motive and knowing one's audience: if the motive is to hurt others or raise yourself above others at their expense, then the line should probably stay behind your lips. If just one who will hear the joke might take offense to it, then it should be filed in the "Do Not Tell Out Loud" folder.

The Bottom Line

Jesus said, "Let the little children come to me" (Matt. 19:14) because He knew how much we'd love listening to those little people.

As a writing teacher, I must admit that my long-suffering suffers through many long afternoons when I have stacks and stacks of 500-word essays to read, but occasionally I'll get a piece of "wisdom" or "nonsense" that makes me laugh so hard I have to stand up before I fall down.

I truly do love freshman theology, philosophy, and inability to type well.

Not one to be outwitted by wits half my size, however, I love to get in the last word with a marginal counterpoint. Here are a few of my favorites.

"Jesus looked down from the Cross upon His executors." (Is that why He said, "Not my *will* but thy *will* be done"?)

"Their excitement in Christ sent chili's up and down my spine." (I thought your vertebra looked kind of red and green.)

"The Lord was calling him to teach, so he went back to school to get rectified." (At the local rectory, I suppose.)

"Breaking relationships with God is not to discredit the evil power of satin." (And I thought spandex was evil.)

"Idle hands are the Devil's warehouse." (I guess that means he's expanding his workshop.)

"I tried to match the names of famous people in the Bible, such as God, Jesus, and some of His decibels." (Say what? Can you speak up?)

"When two people are together and their morals are different, it is what the Bible calls 'uneven yolk.' An evenly matched yolk can result in a fun-filled ride." (Isn't this scrambling Scripture just a bit?)

"Everyone is a free mall agent." (Shop till you drop, buddy!)

"In today's culture, Jesus would wear a plain white T-shirt and a pair of holy jeans." (And his Levi's would be called "Matthews.")

"Jesus asked me to feel His sheep." (No, He didn't!)

"He centers his life around Christ and putting otters first." (That earns my seal of approval.)

"The only thing we have forever is our soles." (But those leather uppers are worthless.)

"The soul-owner is Mr. Rogers." (Get me out of his neighborhood.)

"Preachers in big churches are usually in their middle ages." (And that's why the King James Version is still used.)

"The rich man beeps his faith in God." (Is that what I hear going off two or three times every service?)

"We were all given a candle and we lit it off the person next to us." (This is especially effective in Flint, Michigan.)

"Once you get off the phone, your roommate wants to know all about the conversion." (Ah-ha—televangelism at its best!)

"Charles Darwin believed traits of people were in bread." (Isn't that transubstantiation?)

"I was raised in the Bile Belt." (That makes me reflux, man.)

"The rabbi has everything he wants: friends, respect, and influenza." (Certainly nothing to sneeze at.)

"Monks copied a book or manuscript and then pasted the original onto another monk." (Did the manuscript say, "Kick me"?)

"Before prayer was taken out of school in 1962, many women had babies." (Seems like another good reason to get prayer back in there.)

"Mission Crusaders: remember that Sunday morning has been canceled." (Now if they could just do something about those lousy Monday mornings.)

"We wish to thank the Brunswick, Wiscasset, and Augusta churches for stalking our cupboards and our children." (Stalking 101 seems to be a new course at seminary.)

"Marriage is a sacred vowel." (Especially for Vanna White.)

(Reprinted by permission, *Holiness Today,* June 1, 2003.)

10—what would Jesus eat?

A Christian Response to Nutrition, Obesity, and Eating Disorders

The Scripture

Therefore I tell you, do not worry about your life, what you will eat or drink; or about your body, what you will wear. Is not life more important than food, and the body more important than clothes? Look at the birds of the air; they do not sow or reap or store away in barns, and yet your heavenly Father feeds them. Are you not much more valuable than they? Who of you by worrying can add a single hour to his life? . . .

So do not worry, saying, "What shall we eat?" or "What shall we drink?" or "What shall we wear?" For the pagans run after all these things, and your heavenly Father knows that you need them. But seek first his kingdom and his righteousness, and all these things will be given to you as well. Therefore, do not worry about tomorrow, for tomorrow will worry about itself. Each day has enough trouble of its own (Matt. 6:25-27, 31-34).

The Discussion

Most people in the world eat only to satisfy their hunger; Americans, on the other hand, eat until they're full, until they can't swallow another bite.

And then they have dessert.

In a land of plenty, of plenty more than plenty, of supercenters and mammoth markets, of abundance bordering on opulence, consuming food has become an industry in and of itself. From cooking shows to recipe books, from "Would you like fries with that?" to "Our special tonight is Surf 'n' Turf for $48.95," from electric woks to gas grills, from farming to trucking to sacking and delivering, Americans today are totally obsessed with eating.

And it's beginning to show. According to some recent studies, America has become one of the fattest nations on earth; estimates range as high as half of the population is grossly overweight, and the numbers have been rising over the past three decades. Interestingly, it's not the wealthy who are most affected by overeating; poor people, who tend to eat more processed and packaged food and less fresh food—in part due to prices and in part due to lack of storage and refrigeration mechanisms—tend to fight obesity more. While the rich can afford to buy fresh fruits and vegetables, leaner meats and fewer starches, poor people eat boxes of macaroni and cheese, potato chips, hamburger, and cheap, sugary drinks because that's all they can afford. It fills the stomach, but it eventually turns into layers and layers of fat.

According to the International Obesity Task Force, "The current obesity pandemic reflects the profound changes to society over the past 20 or 30 years that have created an environment that promotes a sedentary lifestyle and the consumption of a high fat, energy dense diet" (www.obesite.chaire.ulaval.ca/iotf.htm). It's not just Americans who battle the bulge three times a day, either. Prevalence of obesity in Europe has increased 10 to 40 percent over the past 10 years. In Japan, obesity in men has doubled in the past 20 years. In 1991, 75 percent of urban men in Western Samoa were considered obese. Even in Africa, where *undernourishment* is horrific, 44 percent of the black women in the Cape Peninsular of the Republic of South Africa are obese (IOTF).

Unfortunately, the word "diet," once existent in only western, industrialized nations, is now being introduced into the lexicons of third world, underdeveloped cultures, as well. This is due, primarily, to the medical complications caused by obesity: respiratory and muscular problems, sleep apnea, osteoarthritis, gout, diabetes, hypertension, strokes, bowel, rectal and stomach cancers, and various other diseases—many potentially fatal. As a result, the costs of medical care and medical insurance associated with the fight against these diseases have skyrocketed over this same time period, now nearing $100 billion annually. Tragically, the mortality rate of young people at the prime of life, 25 to 35 years old, is 12 times higher among the severely obese than it is for lean individuals (IOTF).

Now there are all sorts of methods to discover if one is overweight, obese, or even underweight, ranging from simple waist size, to waist-to-hip ratios, to body mass indexes. Consulting a personal physician is probably the most accurate way to determine whether or not one is obese, but according to the IOTF, men with waists bigger than 40 inches and women with waists bigger than 35 inches are obese. Furthermore, a waist-to-hip measurement ratio in men greater than 90 percent, 80 percent for women, is considered at risk. And according to the body mass index, 25 to 29.9 is considered overweight while anything over 30 is obese.

Obesity is not simply a problem of taking in too many calories; it's also a by-product of not burning off enough calories. As our bodies stop moving at a pace once deemed normal or necessary, as leisure time increases, as people become more active on-line and less active between the lines, metabolic rates slow to frighteningly low levels. And as our metabolism slows down, fat becomes a much more prevalent problem. A healthy balance, of course, is found by increasing physical activity and decreasing caloric intake until you begin to burn as many calories each day as you take in. Not easy, of course, but as they say in training camps all across America, "No Pain, No Gain (or maybe, "No Pain, No Loss").

Another downside to our society's obsession with eating is the alarming rise of eating disorders, especially among women. Although this phenomenon, too, is a symptom related to the overabundance of food, it is also a direct result of body-imaging put forth by today's media, particularly those involved with advertising. Whether it's bulimia, the disorder associated with bingeing and purging, or anorexia nervosa, the obsession for thinness, 90 percent of the victims of eating disorders are women.

In our culture, women are to a great extent asked (some might even say forced) to attain a physique that is completely unnatural in order to ascend the corporate ladder or be accepted in society. To this end, women experience tremendous pressure to attain a certain body form that emphasizes a small waist, large breasts, and impossibly long, shapely legs. As a result, women are highly vulnerable to low self-esteem, depression, anxiety, loneliness, and an obsession with perfection. Because they are frequently judged more on appearance than on their talents and skills, women tend to view themselves as physical creatures, worthy in the world only if they are deemed pretty or desirable by the opposite sex. When this is coupled with family dysfunction, history of abuse or ridicule, difficulty in expressing feelings, or unrealistic expectations for achievement, eating disorders are often the result (Eating Disorder Referral and Information Center, www.edreferral.com).

Victims become withdrawn, obsessed with what they eat—classifying foods as "safe" or "dangerous"—exercise continually, spend inordinate amounts of time in the bathroom, lose their hair and natural skin tone, suffer dizziness and sore throats, suffer diarrhea or constipation, can't sleep or get warm, suffer low blood pressure, and show greater than normal mood swings ("Something Fishy," www.somthing-fishy.org).

Christians are immune to neither obesity nor eating disorders. In fact, some denominations are so concerned with avoiding traditional vices, such as smoking tobacco and drinking alcohol, that they completely ignore the "deadly sin" of gluttony. How many church functions have you been to lately without bumping your thigh against a buffet table full of fried chicken, mashed potatoes, baked beans, potato salad, and chocolate cake? How many Sunday School classes today begin without a trip to the coffee urn, next to which sits a platter of Krispy Kreme doughnuts and cream cheese bagels? How many of our preachers rest their midsections on the pulpit while they rail against the cigarette and beer bottle, gasping for breath, anticipating the Hungry Heifer Smorgasbord down the street? How many youth group facilities include a vending machine of sodas or candy bars? Or both?

And how many of us end every meal by talking about the next meal on the day's agenda?

Jesus was neither obese nor bulimic. For Him, food was merely a means to an end, either a social tool to introduce the Good News of the kingdom of God to a group of unbelievers or a necessary fuel to get Him through the day. It was clearly not His number one priority. (Imagine Him, rising before the sun, saying out loud, "Well, I'm so hungry, I could eat a horse. I wonder what the boys are cookin' up for breakfast this morning.") Yes, some of His most memorable miracles were associated with food: feeding the 5,000 and turning water into wine, to name a couple, but He always used food as metaphor, symbolizing some aspect of God's kingdom or His Father's unwavering love. Or He simply ate what was available and moved on.

In his book, *The What Would Jesus Eat Cook Book* (Thomas Nelson Publishers, Nashville, 2002), Don Colbert, M.D., states that "the eating habits that were the foundation of Jesus' diet were choosing untampered, nutrient-dense foods; avoiding foods that [had] been processed or refined; choosing foods that [were] in their natural, fresh state" (ix). Jesus was not a Twinkie/Dr. Pepper kind of guy; He was much more apt to snack on a handful of fresh nuts, even some barley grains, and down it with a ladle of boiled and cooled lake or stream water (no ice). Undoubtedly, Jesus ate bread that had been cooked that same day, brown rice, and fresh fish. He would have rarely had or taken the opportunity to eat beef or chicken, or dined on anything too sweet or too rich. As a nomad who lived among the poor of the land, His diet would have been just enough to keep His body moving forward.

Here are some of the steps Colbert suggests one might take to adopt a healthier eating lifestyle, one that aligns itself quite closely to what Jesus would have eaten in His day and might continue to eat today.

1. Eliminate processed foods from your cupboards and start over. Buy whole grain products and fresh fruits and vegetables. Stock your shelves with olive oil, nuts, seeds, and whole grains.

2. Cook and bake with whole grain products. Eat more fresh fruits, vegetables, beans, legumes, and nuts.

3. Substitute olive oil for butter, margarine, salad dressings, and all other oils.

4. Avoid all fried foods.

5. Limit cheeses to Parmesan and feta. Never eat a block of cheese.

6. Eat yogurt with fruit or sweeten it with Stevia (a natural sugar substitute).

7. Choose fish and poultry over red meat. Eat meat sparingly. Cut out sugary sweets.

8. Exercise regularly. Walk more.

9. Make dining an experience you enjoy with others. Slow down your eating. Savor your food and enjoy sharing life with family and friends *(ix-x)*.

The Bottom Line

We have got to stop eating so much. And we have to start exercising more. Much, much more. It seems that we have replaced the golden calf of Old Testament idolaters with the glazed ham, au gratin potatoes, and enough pecan pie to feed 5,000. That's not to say we shouldn't enjoy eating or preparing meals for our friends and family. It's not even suggesting that doughnuts stop showing up in Sunday School classes across America.

It simply means we should stop eating until we get so full we can hardly scoot our chairs away from the table and stumble over to the couch for a midafternoon nap. We should stop putting convenient food on the table rather than compassionate food. We should begin to emphasize the fellowship of the meal rather than the fodder-fare of the meal. We should remove as much sugar and salt from the kitchen as we can. We should buy fresh, bake fresh, and serve fresh instead of buying box after box, bag after bag of processed food.

According to the National Institutes of Health, we need to buy and eat the following:

Fat-free or low-fat milk, yogurt, cheese, and cottage cheese
Light or diet margarine (or olive oil)
Egg substitutes
Bagels and pita bread
Soft corn tortillas
Low-fat and low-sodium crackers
Plain cereals
Dry beans and peas
Skinless chicken/turkey white meat
Unbattered fish
Lean beef (when you just have to have beef)
Fresh, frozen, or canned fruit (in light syrup)
Fresh, frozen, or canned vegetables (no salt)
Low-fat or nonfat salad dressing (or olive oil)
Herbs and spices
Salsa (www.shlbi.nih.gov)
And while we're eating more healthfully, we should walk

as many errands as we can. If we live close to work, school, or church (three miles or fewer), we should get up earlier and take the time to walk. Towns and cities should insist on building more sidewalks and bike lanes to encourage motorless travel. And instead of joining an expensive health spa so you can walk 10 miles on a treadmill, just walk the 5 miles to the spa's front door, turn around, walk home, and put your $40 membership fee in the offering plate this Sunday. (Right next to the plate of doughnuts.)

And remember Dr. Colbert's bit of eating wisdom: "Breakfast like a king; lunch like a prince; dinner like a pauper" (vii).

11—what would Jesus drink?

A Christian Response to Alcohol and Sugary Beverages

The Scripture

On the third day a wedding took place at Cana in Galilee. Jesus' mother was there, and Jesus and his disciples had also been invited to the wedding. When the wine was gone, Jesus' mother said to him, "They have no more wine."

"Dear woman, why do you involve me?" Jesus replied. "My time has not yet come."

His mother said to the servants, "Do whatever he tells you."

Nearby stood six stone water jars, the kind used by the Jews for ceremonial washing, each holding from twenty to thirty gallons.

Jesus said to the servants, "Fill the jars with water"; so they filled them to the brim.

Then he told them, "Now draw some out and take it to the master of the banquet."

They did so, and the master of the banquet tasted the water that had been turned into wine. He did not realize where it had come from, though the servants who had drawn the water knew. Then he called the bridegroom aside and said, "Everyone brings out the choice wine first and then the cheaper wine after the guests have had too much to drink; but you have saved the best till now" (John 2:1-10).

The Discussion

There is a great denominational divide over the issue of alcohol consumption: many churches believe that drinking anything that has been fermented or otherwise has become alcoholic is morally offensive to God, while some religious groups teach that it's OK. On which side of the divide would Jesus land?

Philip Lancaster has written an article for *Patriarch Magazine* in which he studies how differences in doctrine—in how the Holy Scripture is interpreted—can influence a church body. Lancaster says that "because God is its author, there is one correct meaning to any portion of Scripture. God is not confused. When He speaks, He speaks truth, and that truth is not confused or self-contradictory. A passage means exactly what He meant when He spoke it through the inspired writer. It is true that some passages may have multiple layers of meaning and application, but these are all part of the one meaning He attached to them" (www.patriarchspath.org).

This is the fundamentalist viewpoint on the inerrancy of the Bible: one meaning originally, one meaning today. It is this claim of "multiple layers of meaning and application" that may allow for denominational divisions over doctrine, however.

Lancaster further suggests that "understanding Bible doctrine [truth] is a corporate, not an individual process" (www.patriarchspath.org). Although an individual can be inspired by the Holy Spirit to interpret Scripture, it is the teachability of the individual that makes for necessary corporate learning. "Since no one Christian, being still darkened by sin, can presume infallibility when interpreting a passage of Scripture, believers need to submit to one another and in humility receive instruction, so that the whole body can together grow in its understanding of truth," Lancaster states.

When done in a personal position of humility, instruction unites rather than divides. It is only when we become pious and proud that teaching or learning must attempt to overcome the spiritual vacuum resulting from anger, derision, or division.

Clearly, if someone belongs to a denomination—Church of the Nazarene, Baptist, Pentecostal, or some other—that opposes the drinking of alcohol, he or she has a responsibility to be true to that denomination. When we join a church, we promise to be faithful to the lifestyle it values. That's what it means to be in a covenant, and joining a church places a person in a covenant with others. Plus, the New Testament teaches that Christians are not to be stumbling blocks for their weaker companions. So, if we are in a denomination that has taken a stand against drinking and we choose to disregard this, we not only tarnish our integrity but also risk harming others. And that is surely not in harmony with Jesus' commandment to love one another, which is part of the greater covenant that we have with Him.

With this in mind, what can we say about alcohol alone? As discussed in other chapters, the idea of enhancing the health of the human body, the "temple of the Holy Spirit," seems solidly supported in Scripture. Whether through exercise or balanced nutrition, it would appear that whatever improves one's overall health is endorsed by God. Some contend that the consumption of moderate amounts of alcohol improves one's health. "A mountain of scientific evidence is building up to support the contention that two glasses of red wine a day have beneficial health results," according to an article on *The Winemaking Home Page,* titled, "The Potential Health Benefits of Red Wine Consumption." "From the prevention of neurodegenerative diseases such as Alzheimer's and Parkinson's disease to the prevention of cardiovascular diseases, from preventing food poisoning, dysentery, and so-called 'traveler's diarrhea' to reduction in human mortality rates, the benefits of red wine consumption are piling up," the article goes on to say.

One might expect this sort of rhetoric from winemakers, but the evidence from less-biased groups seems to support this finding. "Research scientists in North Carolina have announced discovery of how a chemical found in red wine helps to fight cancer," according to CNN. "The new research identified the workings of a key cancer-related substance: trans-Resveratrol, often called Res. In addition to red grapes, Res is found in mulberries, raspberries, peanuts, muscadine grapes including scuppernongs, and many other fruits and nuts" (www.cnn.com).

"Researchers at Northwestern University Medical School have found that a chemical in red wine believed to help reduce risk for heart disease is a form of estrogen. The substance, resveratrol, is highly concentrated in the skin of grapes and is abundant in red wine," according to an article in *Science Daily*. "Resveratrol protects grapes and some other plants against fungal infections. It has . . . a number of potentially beneficial properties, including antioxidant, anticoagulant, anti-inflammatory, and anti-cancer effects" (www.sciencedaily.com).

Not everyone adheres to the theory that there are significant health benefits to drinking alcohol. One study even reports that the findings concerning the benefits of drinking red wine may be tainted by the fact that those who drink red wine normally eat an overall healthier diet—one full of fruits, fresh vegetables, fish, and less saturated fat—than the general population. "Some of the real benefit may be in the cuisine associated with wine drinking—a traditionally 'Mediterranean' diet and one that is found in many French homes" (www.cnn.com). The *British Medical Journal* gives credence to this argument, citing France's diet that is unusually low in animal fat and cholesterol as the main contributor to the country's relatively low incidence of heart disease.

The University of Wisconsin Medical School in Madison found in its 1999 study that one could get the same positive health benefits of red wine in nonalcoholic purple grape juice. "Purple grape juice contains the same powerful disease-fighting anti-oxidents, called flavonoids, that are believed to give wine many of its heart-friendly benefits" (www.cnn.com).

The harmful effects of drinking alcohol seem to outweigh whatever benefits it might have. The American Cancer Society says that a woman's risk of breast cancer goes up if she drinks alcohol (www.cnn.com). The U.S. Department of Justice reports that "alcohol abuse was a factor in 40 percent of violent crimes committed in the United States" ("Violence and Alcohol," U.S.J.D. Report on Alcohol and Crime). And the number of alcoholics in the United States is growing at an alarming rate. "Not once, in all of history," writes John Todd, M.D., in his book, *The Doctor's Terrific Tablets*, has "a human individual . . . started consuming alcohol with the deliberate plan of causing himself to become an 'alcoholic.' And yet, in the United States, today, there are at least 15 million overt alcoholics—and many, many more 'borderline' alcoholics" (www.terrific-tabs.com). As one might contend with any habit, if you don't take the first drink, it's hard to become a victim of alcohol.

Alcoholism, also called Alcohol Dependence Syndrome, is all about uncontrolled craving that brings about physical dependence that only gets stronger as the patient continues to drink. As time goes on, more alcohol is needed to retain its effects on the alcoholic. Even those who drink great amounts of alcohol but are not considered alcoholics can do long-term damage to their bodies. "Young people who binge drink could be risking serious damage to their brains now and increasing memory loss later in adulthood," according to the article, "Lacking an Original Thought Just Now?" published in the latest issue of *Alcoholism: Clinical and Experimental Research* (alcoholism.about.com). When we consider the potentially devastating effects on health and family, we would do well to heed these warnings.

When it comes to unhealthy drinks, though, alcohol is not the only culprit. Soda has been linked to obesity, tooth decay, softening of bone tissue, and caffeine dependence. A group of researchers out of Harvard University found that "12-year-olds who drank soft drinks regularly were more likely to be overweight than those who didn't. For each additional daily serving of sugar-sweetened soft drink consumed during the nearly two-year study, the risk of obesity increased 1.6 times" (Sally Squires, *Washington Post,* February 27, 2001). Moreover, the sugar and other acids in soda pop "are notorious for etching tooth enamel in ways that can lead to cavities, according to the Ohio Dental Association. The phosphorus found in soda can "deplete bones of calcium." And finally, dependence on caffeine from soft drinks can cause splitting headaches, high blood pressure, irritability, and even stomach problems (Squires).

The Bottom Line

Did Jesus drink wine? There is really no way to know for certain. Grape juice and wine would have been staple drinks of His culture and time, so if He did, indeed, socialize with people in His culture, then He was possibly served wine on occasion. In Luke's Gospel, Jesus says, "John the Baptist came neither eating bread nor drinking wine, and you say, 'He has a demon.' The Son of Man came eating and drinking, and you say, 'Here is a glutton and a drunkard, a friend of tax collectors and 'sinners'" (7:33). A cup of wine was served at the Last Supper. Many of the Master's parables were set in vineyards and included references to winepresses and wine goblets. Just the history of refrigeration implies to us that whatever juice was made from grapes at that time possibly fermented before it was consumed.

Did Jesus ever drink too much wine? Certainly not. Given what is told to us about Jesus in Scripture, we can surmise that. He never overdid anything, whether it was eating, exercising, sleeping, preaching, healing, or drinking. His life was one of moderation and balance. Scripture is full of scathing language for drunkards.

What would Jesus drink today? Given the options that He would have today—purified, clean water, especially—He would likely make the socially responsible and healthy choice to drink water, juice, milk, and the like. Again, this is an "interpretation of scriptural truth" that might be better served by the corporate denomination than the individual. If you belong to a body of believers whose denominational stance is abstinence, then the appropriate life choice is obvious—abstinence.

Would Jesus drink even a Coke once in a while? Probably. But, given His omniscience or even His awareness of current events, if He knew the money earned by any soft drink company were going to support any unsavory activities, He would definitely find it difficult to support such expenditures. It is not likely that He would drink a sugary, caffeine-laden soft drink at every meal or on every break. For that same reason, He would probably avoid the morning habit of a cup of coffee, much less a whole morning or day of drinking so much caffeine. He knew the long-term benefits of being well rested and calm-natured.

Would Jesus spring for bottled water rather than drinking tap water or fresh water from a stream or well? We've already established that Jesus would not have had a lot of money in His pockets—and if He did, He wouldn't think of himself first when He spent it—so it's difficult to imagine His carrying around with Him an Evian water bottle everywhere He went. What is fairly certain is that He would drink a healthy amount of water every day, wherever and whenever He could get it.

Jesus said, "What goes into a man's mouth does not make him 'unclean,' but what comes out of his mouth, that is what makes him 'unclean'" (Matt. 15:11). Followers of Jesus Christ must be sure that nothing they eat or drink becomes a matter of excess or an idol—the focus of one's attention, an obsession that controls one's actions or decisions. Where alcohol is concerned, the evidence is compelling: abstinence is the best choice. But if any beverage (even coffee or soda) begins to overtake one's life, Jesus would advise its victim to abstain from that as well.

12—how would Jesus protest?

A Christian Response to Social Activism

The Scripture

"Stand up, plead your case before the mountains; let the hills hear what you have to say. Hear, O mountains, the LORD's accusation; listen, you everlasting foundations of the earth. For the LORD has a case against his people; he is lodging a charge against Israel.

"My people, what have I done to you? How have I burdened you? Answer me. I brought you up out of Egypt and redeemed you from the land of slavery. I sent Moses to lead you, also Aaron and Miriam. My people, remember what Balak king of Moab counseled and what Balaam son of Beor answered. Remember your journey from Shittim to Gilgal, that you may know the righteous acts of the LORD."

With what shall I come before the LORD and bow down before the exalted God? Shall I come before him with burnt offerings, with calves a year old? Will the LORD be pleased with thousands of rams, with ten thousand rivers of oil? Shall I offer my firstborn for my transgression, the fruit of my body for the sin of my soul? He has showed you, O man, what is good. And what does the LORD require of you? To act justly and to love mercy and to walk humbly with your God (Micah 6:1-8).

The Discussion

"To act justly."
"To love mercy."
"To walk humbly with your God."

With these three admonitions, the prophet Micah lays the scriptural foundation for the (righteous) method of social activism for every follower of Jesus Christ. And it seems highly appropriate that it is Micah, whose very name means "Who is like Yahweh?" who should lay this foundation. It was during the time frame of this Old Testament book that Syria, Judah, Samaria, and Israel were all being conquered and annexed by pagan Assyria. Micah claims in his writings that these events are to be interpreted as both omens of doom *and* hopeful signs of God's eternal faithfulness. According to the translators of the *New International Version* of the Bible, "Micah stresses that God hates idolatry, injustice, rebellion and empty ritualism, but he delights in pardoning the penitent" (*NIV Study Bible,* 1371).

To read Micah, then, is to read a foreshadowing of our world today. From the headlines and news bulletins of media to the political manipulation of governments around the globe, people continue to wallow between the gloom of inevitable Armageddon and the promise of loving redemption. Indeed, there are wars and rumors of wars being broadcast every day through today's "24/7" media blitz. It is this obsession with information, unfortunately, that feeds our phobias, even among Christians, and, therefore, intensifies our resolve to become cultural change-agents for God's great mission. After all, the reasoning goes, "If we don't make a difference here and now, where and when and who will?"

Social activism takes many forms and wears many faces, many of which are far more destructive, ultimately, than the very issues that have initiated the activism in the first place. One wouldn't need to look beyond groups like the Ku Klux Klan, the Michigan Militia and Operation Rescue to see how far astray some people go in attempting to "put feet to God's word." All of these fanatical organizations began and continue to operate under the illusion that they are "acting justly, loving mercy and walking humbly with their God."

The results of their activities, however, aren't anything close to justice, mercy, or humility.

Operation Rescue, for instance, has taken *credit* for many of the attacks on abortion clinics across the United States in recent years, justifying these acts as *fighting a war against evil,* at least the subjective definition of evil of some of its membership. The Michigan Militia is just one of many privately funded armies of weapons and propaganda in this country that attempt to sabotage the government of the United States, particularly concerning the *defense* of individual liberties. And the KKK, that notorious collection of "sanctified racists," was founded on the principle of doing God's work for the white race, by whatever means it takes, including but not limited to lynching, bombing, and arson.

During the summer of 2003, the nation's eyes were riveted to a state courthouse in Alabama where a small group of citizens, led by one of the state's Supreme Court justices who continually professed his allegiance to the laws of Almighty God above the laws he had once sworn to defend, gathered on the courthouse steps to protect and preserve the granite display of the Ten Commandments. For weeks, the evening news and the glut of talk shows it has spawned showed and then discussed the actions of these people, prostrated in prayer and pumped with purpose, shouting "Amen" and "Glory be to God," as they attempted to merge their Christian faith with their Constitutional freedom.

The Church and the country, naturally, split down the middle on this issue and the subsequent action of the people involved. Some saw these Christian citizens as modern-day Micahs, doing whatever was necessary to ensure that God was represented in the halls of American justice. Others, however, wondered if the graying of the separation of Church and State did not serve as a frightening preamble to the religious fanaticism that seems to be at the center of conflict in so much of the Middle East. While the judge's apologists defended his action as a lightning rod of faithful-

ness to God's truth, his detractors viewed him as a dangerous storm on the horizon, a hypocrite to both his faith and
his elected position.

This dilemma, which every citizen and Christian faces at
some point in his or her life, is difficult to resolve. Whether
the issue is abortion or pornography, gay rights or war,
capital punishment or gun control, each of us will take a
different route to demonstrating both our citizenship and
our discipleship. At the core of our actions, however, whatever they are, is that penetrating and permeating question,
"What would Jesus do?"

The Bottom Line

To deny that Jesus himself was a social activist is not only
naive but also a significant misreading of the New Testament. He was a mover and shaker of the highest order, re-
versing and inverting much of the social stratification and
hierarchy of His day. Remember, it was Jesus who said, "But
many who are first will be last, and many who are last will
be first" (Matt. 19:30); "If anyone wants to be first, he must
be the very last, and the servant of all" (Mark 9:35); "You
have heard that it was said, 'Love your neighbor and hate
your enemy.' But I tell you: Love your enemies and pray for
those who persecute you" (Matt. 5:43-44); "You have heard
that it was said, 'Eye for eye, and tooth for tooth.' But I tell
you, Do not resist an evil person. If someone strikes you on
the right cheek, turn to him the other also" (vv. 38-39). The
Gospel accounts are full of such moral, ethical, and cultural
transpositions. After all, in a world of injustice, Jesus
demonstrated justice; in a world of war, Jesus advocated
peace; in a world of violence and vengeance, Jesus showed
mercy; in a world of greed, Jesus lived humbly.

How, then, did Jesus choose His battles? How did He
decide which issues were important and which weren't?
How did He measure what truly mattered? It would be easy
to contend that Jesus did *not* choose His battles—His bat-

tles chose Him! In nearly every case in Scripture where Jesus teaches, preaches, or acts on a social level, He is *responding* to an inquiry or *reacting* to an inequity. He does not necessarily seek conflict, but He never shies away from it, either. He addresses it with both authority and sincere humility—not an easy combination.

Jesus was the Liberator of the oppressed and the Advocate of the neglected. Where He saw injustice, His response was at once quick and certain. He disdained hypocrisy, especially in Church leadership: "Woe to you Pharisees, because you give God a tenth of your mint, rue and all other kinds of garden herbs, but you neglect justice and the love of God. You should have practiced the latter without leaving the former undone" (Luke 11:42). In other words, Jesus is condemning the piety of adhering to the letter of the law when practiced in complete disregard of the essence of the law, which is love and justice.

Jesus could not—and would not—tolerate any kind of discrimination or sanctioned inequality, especially when based on greed or creed: "Do not judge, or you too will be judged. For in the same way you judge others, you will be judged, and with the measure you use, it will be measured to you. Why do you look at the speck of sawdust in your brother's eye and pay no attention to the plank in your own eye? How can you say to your brother, 'Let me take the speck out of your eye,' when all the time there is a plank in your own eye? You hypocrite, first take the plank out of your own eye, and then you will see clearly to remove the speck from your brother's eye" (Matt. 7:1-5).

Jesus was concerned with the heart's intent as much as with any external behavior. "You have heard that it was said to the people long ago, 'Do not murder, and anyone who murders will be subject to judgment.' But I tell you that anyone who is angry with his brother will be subject to judgment" (5:21-22); and "You have heard that it was said, 'Do not commit adultery.' But I tell you that anyone who looks at a woman lustfully has already committed adultery with her in his heart" (vv. 27-28).

The 20th century gave us three excellent models of how Jesus would protest: Mahatma Gandhi, the Hindu spiritual leader whose humble yet powerful lifestyle led to Indian independence; Mother Teresa, the Catholic nun who dedicated her life to the neglected people of Calcutta; and Martin Luther King, the Baptist preacher whose social activism led to the Civil Rights Movement of the 1950s and 1960s. All three advocated nonviolence, even when horribly assaulted by those who held the power in government. All three held to a tenet of passive resistance that turned the other cheek and met evil with good. And all three actively sought the leadership of the divine, praying with their followers for wisdom and grace.

Perhaps they, then, as well as Jesus, provide the model for our own social activism. First and foremost, we should always act out of sincere concern and compassion, never hatred or some sort of misdirected fanatical passion. Yes, as many will readily point out, Jesus showed human anger in the Temple when He overthrew the merchants and scam artists, but that event was obviously the exception to His personality, not the rule. Jesus typically handled himself with restraint and love—always love. His natural demeanor was serene and gracious, embracing the lonely and encouraging the dejected.

Whenever possible, our social activism should be private and quiet, not calling undue attention to ourselves or our so-called causes. This is not to suggest that public demonstrations or mass passive resistance is always inappropriate—not at all; however, to "perform" on the street corner when writing a letter or making a phone call would be equally effective wastes a lot of energy that could be more efficiently used.

At the university setting, for instance, many students who feel wronged by the administration or school's rules often want to strike back in a public forum such as the campus newspaper or a chapel address or a dormitory petition. In their immaturity and need for immediate self-gratification, they think that publicly raking someone over the coals is a highly effective way of getting their way. Their thinking is that if they can bring someone of authority down to their level, they will, in turn, rise in the campus hierarchy. Good advice to them is always (1) put yourself in the other person's shoes when you think about what happened; (2) pray for the person you are seeking to harm, by name; and (3) do what you can to resolve this matter privately.

We should not protest for personal gain or to win those individual rights that would cause innocent people to suffer. This takes careful research and intuitive planning. Scientists tell us that for every action, there is an equal reaction; we must consider, then, what reaction our initial action will cause. If Side A wins the battle, let's say, not only should we consider what happens to Side B, but we should also consider the Side Cs and Side Ds that are not in the immediate picture. This is at the core of the debate over environmental issues. If this nation does this action today, then it is wise to ask what will happen to that nation on that other side of the world 200 years from now? If we turn that national forest into an oil field to satisfy today's economy, what effect will that have on our grandchildren? If we protest for lower grocery prices, what will that do to those who work in agriculture or trucking?

Finally, we should always look at issues through the telescope of eternity rather than the microscope of immediacy, mistranslating the urgent into the truly important. In other words, we should ask whether our actions will lead to long-lasting human benefits or short-term satisfaction. Is whether or not a 5,000-pound stone facsimile of Exod. 20:2-17 remains on the steps of the courthouse going to make an eternal difference in the kingdom of God? Is that what we want our lives to stand for? Does that stone matter to God?

Moreover, when it comes right down to it, isn't taking the life of a doctor or nurse who performs abortions simply choosing whose life is sacred and whose life isn't? Does God ever sanction murder, no matter what its motive might be? Does God equate a dozen infant lives with one doctor's life?

Furthermore, does the demand "to bear arms" or to execute a murderer reflect our true understanding of God's mercy and grace, especially as He has shown us His mercy and grace through His Son, Jesus? Can we see our Savior on the cross of Calvary, suffering untold pain and torture on our behalf, then turn around and say to the prisoner on His right, "Christ never died for you, man. He died for good people like me"?

Remember, in all things, it is wise to confess: "I am the chief of sinners."

13—what would Jesus say about . . . ?

Quick Christian Responses to Various Social Issues

Euthanasia

The ability and technology human beings now possess to heal each other and kill each other boggle the mind. Medical science has advanced at such a pace that cultural ethics have a hard time keeping up. "Mercy killing," once the bailiwick solely of veterinarian medicine, has now become an issue in hospitals, hospices, and family living rooms.

There are two types of euthanasia: active and passive. Active euthanasia is really what veterinarians do to terminally ill or horribly injured animals. Using an intravenous line or hypodermic needle, the doctor injects a lethal toxin into the blood system of the animal; within seconds, the animal dies painlessly. Nonmedical individuals, unexpectedly faced with a dying animal, might resort to more primitive but equally effective methods, such as a gunshot or blow to the head.

Passive euthanasia is a bit more complicated. This is normally the type considered by medical personnel when dealing with terminally ill or injured patients. People! Passive euthanasia is characterized by deprivation of life-sustaining measures: nourishment, respiratory machinery, chemicals, or perhaps even surgical procedures. Terms like "DNR—do not resuscitate," "brain dead," and "living wills" are associated closely to passive euthanasia.

Jesus did not wish any individual to suffer in life, even in dying. His words and actions throughout the Gospels have the undercurrent of comforting the uncomfortable and relieving the pain of the suffering. He also valued the sacredness of life. Would He advocate active euthanasia? Probably not. Would He support passive euthanasia? Maybe, depending on the circumstances. Unlike you and me, however, Jesus had healing powers that may make this a moot point altogether.

War

This is a topic often mired in patriotic fervor. Because the United States is a democracy that emphasizes both the *right* of the individual and the *responsibility* of its citizenry to protect those rights, a person might be able to make a valid Christian argument for or against war.

The Bible is not shy when it comes to revealing God's use of conflict in exacting His will on the people, particularly in the Old Testament, where there are 32 such references. Jesus, on the other hand, mentions war only once: "When you hear of wars and rumors of wars, do not be alarmed. Such things must happen, but the end is still to come. Nation will rise against nation, and kingdom against kingdom" (Mark 13:7-8). He alludes to war (at least to hand-to-hand conflict) one other time, in Matt. 26:52: "Put your sword back in its place, . . . for all who draw the sword will die by the sword."

Does either admonition of Christ indicate whether He was for or against war? It would be comforting to all of us if it were that easy. Because every conflict is different, with different motives, different leaders, different countries, and different potentials, there might not be a single, definitive answer to the question. Yet it does seem clear that Jesus was opposed to violence, both personal and political. Even though He knew wars were inevitable, He would certainly be opposed to the concept of *war* as a means of resolving conflicting ideologies or goals. Does that make every war, therefore, morally wrong?

We'll have to ask Him when we get to heaven.

Health Care

Jesus broke "the law" of His society when it came to administering His own brand of health care, so we mustn't get bogged down with some nationalistic notion that America's health-care system is sacrosanct. Most would admit today's system is flawed.

Staying healthy today costs each individual in the United States thousands of dollars a year, so if a person does not have medical insurance to defray the bulk of what it costs to get treatment, he or she will become a victim rather than a patient. Costs are spiraling out of control, and with each increase in insurance benefits there seems to be an increase in physician or hospital billing.

Because doctors and hospitals have taken oaths to care for everyone in need, nobody who needs medical attention is supposed to be turned away. People who cannot pay their bills are supposed to be given the same care as those who can, so the doctor/hospital absorbs a fraction of the loss, but insurance carriers take most of the financial burden. In the long run, then, those who have personal medical insurance, in essence, pay for those who don't.

Many nations have a national or "universal" health-care system, what its detractors call "socialized medicine." The basic principle is the same as what is happening by default in the United States, but the burden is borne by taxpayers rather than insurance premium-payers.

Jesus would advocate justice in health care. He would work for a system that gave all citizens an equal opportunity to get medical care, whether that was supported by the government or by the church or by a group of compassionate citizens. But He would be offended by a medical system that made some rich at the expense of the poor.

Deforestation

What is happening to the environment is, without question, shortsighted. From the unwillingness to give up a handful of individual rights for the sake of our water, land, and air—not to mention the future of humanity—to the total destruction of unique and life-sustaining habitats, human beings have completely misunderstood God's mandate to "fill the earth and subdue it" (Gen. 1:28).

There are so many viable alternatives available today to what we're doing in the Amazon Rain Forest, for one: cutting down trees that cannot and will not be replaced in time to keep entire species alive. Whether it's houses, businesses, or fuels, the world does not need to destroy these rich habitats in order to "improve" human life.

Jesus would be appalled by what greed is doing to His Father's creation. This is one issue about which there is little question what He would do. He would "fight city hall" to keep natural resources alive and thriving.

Interracial Marriage

To think that Jesus sees color when He looks at His children shows little insight into the heart of God's Son. He spent a great deal of His time on earth, disposing the myth that one person is better or more godly than another, that one nationality is better or more godly than another, that one race is better or more godly than another.

Therefore, interracial marriage is not a spiritual, theological, or biblical issue whatsoever. It is purely a social issue, conceived by one race who did not want to lose its power to another. Unfortunately, this very issue has split Christian homes and church denominations. It even split this nation 150 years ago.

On the one side are those who dare to cite Paul's admonition out of context as support for their claim: "Do not be yoked together with unbelievers" or as it says in the King James Version, "Be ye not unequally yoked together with unbelievers," often conveniently omitting the last two words. Or they quote Judg. 14:3 or Ezra 9:12, applying it to interracial marriages rather than its true context.

The fact of the matter is, if it weren't for marriages that crossed cultures, races, and nationalities, most of us would not even be here to argue the issue.

Cursing

What is the definition of a "bad word"? Is it a word that is inherently evil by its very definition or is it a word censored at home or in school or is it a word that has a negative association or connotation?

The biblical definition of "cursing" has very little in common with this concept of "bad words" and "good words"; rather, Scripture is really referring to *damning* or *condemning* an individual or group of people to an eternity in hell, thereby usurping God's unique role as Judge on judgment day. The Bible is much clearer on patience as a virtue and anger as a vice than it is about the words one utters when frustrated.

On the other hand, the third commandment is quite clear: "You shall not misuse the name of the LORD your God, for the LORD will not hold anyone guiltless who misuses his name" (Exod. 20:7). We call such an act "profanity," but does "profanity" include all epithets or vulgarities?

Jesus told us to let our lights shine in the darkness, so we must ask ourselves the question: does saying that word brighten my light or extinguish my light? The answer will tell us Jesus' opinion of that word.

Tobacco

As with drinking alcohol, this is an issue usually seen as a doctrinal dispute rather than a personal difference of opinion. The medical facts, however, are tough to ignore: smoking kills people. Cigarettes, cigars, pipes, chewing tobacco, snuff, and any other mechanism that puts tar, nicotine, and other toxins into the human body destroy the "temple of the Holy Spirit."

The argument that tobacco has some benefits—smooths out the "rough edges" of stress, keeps one's weight down, or gives the smoker energy—does not overcome the overwhelming data from medical science. The incidence rate of cancer and heart disease is much higher among smokers than nonsmokers.

Added to this is the burden that smokers must bear for causing any number of diseases to nonsmokers via their secondary smoke. Husbands of smokers get emphysema; children of smokers suffer acute asthma; coworkers of smokers are much more prone to respiratory infections.

Jesus would tell smokers to give it up, simply for their own health and the well-being of others. The question of whether smoking is a moral issue is really the same question that should be asked with any addiction, be it food or alcohol or sex or pornography or money.

Divorce

The waters surrounding this issue have certainly muddied over the years, especially in the United States, where just under a million divorces are finalized every year. Citing reasons that range from infidelity to the inability to get along, approximately 40 percent of marriages today end in court (www.divorcereform.org).

The Bible says that only infidelity is a valid reason to break up the marriage contract; in truth, according to Scripture, if the marriage vow to be faithful to one another is broken, then the contract is, in spirit, already broken. The problem is that marriages actually end for many other reasons today, most notably, "irreconcilable differences." Does God recognize such a divorce that may meet American legal standards but does not quite reach His own standard of "adultery only"?

Is a marriage that is characterized by bitterness, stress, alienation, even abuse considered an irreconcilable marriage in the eyes of God? Wouldn't even Jesus find it difficult to advise a victim of verbal, emotional, or physical abuse to stick with such a potentially dangerous "marriage"? The argument that the abusing spouse has, indeed, "committed adultery" with the bottle or the needle or his own temper could sound terribly compelling to the Prince of *Peace.* Is adultery solely sexual?

The question becomes, then, would Jesus put the letter of the law ahead of the essence of the law?

Cloning

It wasn't all that long ago that this procedure was relegated to the Science Fiction Channel on cable television. Then came Dolly.

Ever since scientists were able to "create" a sheep identical to another sheep by genetic manipulation, humanity has been presented with yet another moral and ethical dilemma. Can the manufacture of human tissue through genetic cloning become so overwhelmingly beneficial to the species that any negative consequences are deemed superfluous? Conversely, can genetic engineering and manipulation be today and forevermore considered a pursuit left better in the hands of God Almighty?

Similar questions were raised when other medical milestones were reached: vaccines, birth control, artificial egg-fertilization techniques, even organ transplants. Are we "playing God" when we discover these medical breakthroughs or are we "using the brains God gave us"?

Certainly, proponents of such medical technology could argue that Jesus "cloned" new tissue when He made the lame man walk or the blind man see. Opponents to cloning, however, would call that leap of logic an oversimplified albeit clever act of semantic hocus-pocus.

Whatever one might suppose Jesus would say on this issue, most would agree that it's a question that bears extreme caution.

Fear

Most of us have heard the saying that "faith is the antidote to fear." Some have gone so far as to suggest that fear is "anti-faith." Either is a bit simplistic.

There are some fears that are beneficial to our well-being: the fear of falling, for instance, keeps many potential casualties tucked safely in the back of the line or away from the precipice. The fear of drowning keeps nonswimmers on the land, and the fear of getting a ticket keeps many folks under the speed limit.

Some fears, however, border on the irrational and necessitate therapy with trained professionals. Often, these are a result of chemical imbalances that can be regulated with medicine and cognitive behavioral changes. Sometimes, though, these phobias go untreated and cause great turmoil to their victims.

The idea of fear is discussed through both Testaments of the Bible. The psalmist says that his fears are allayed by the promises of God: "Even though I walk through the valley of the shadow of death, I will fear no evil, for you are with me" (23:4). "The Lord is my light and my salvation—whom shall I fear?" (27:1). "In God, whose word I praise, in God I trust; I will not be afraid" (56:4). Jesus said, "You of little faith, why are you so afraid?" (Matt. 8:26). "Take courage! It is I. Don't be afraid" (14:27). "Don't be afraid; just believe" (Mark 5:36).

Jesus would probably say the same thing today: "God loves you and will ultimately take you in His arms to live with Him forever. So don't be afraid. I will see you there."

Gun Control

Jesus had quite an arsenal at his disposal, 12 legions (approximately 10,000) angels, presumably armed with supernatural weapons, yet he chose to take the path of nonviolence when it came time for his arrest. It seems overly simplistic, perhaps, but the question naturally arises: would Jesus shoot another human being for any reason?

Does Jesus expect Christians to hold themselves to the

same standard of behavior that He held himself? Is it acceptable and scripturally supported to defend our families, our countries, and ourselves with firearms or knives or swords or stones? It's a huge chunk of biblical cud to chew.

Capital Punishment

The Hebrew culture of the Old Testament practiced the death penalty for a number of offenses, including being disrespectful to parents, taking the Lord's name in vain, and adultery. Obviously, today's culture is a bit more tolerant. Even the oft-quoted adage from Moses, "an eye for an eye, a tooth for a tooth," was a call for mercy, to make the punishment fit the crime rather than become too excessive.

Jesus' response to crime or sin was always mercy. The woman caught in adultery was spared when Jesus' indicting sense of reverse justice effectively dispersed the crowd of executioners: "If any of you is without sin, let him be the first to throw a stone at her" (John 8:7). He preached frequently about returning good for evil. Does that mean we ignore the Old Testament in favor of the New? Hardly. It simply means we must interpret the Old Testament through the loving lens of Christ's life and teaching.

Gay Rights

Jesus didn't just live among sinners; He lived *for* sinners to deliver them from their sins and a life of sinning. Whether the sin is bearing false witness (lying and gossiping) or dishonoring parents (neglecting and abusing) or lust (within or between the sexes), Jesus lived and *died* for each of us.

Jesus went to the woman who was condemned by her culture and offered her the keys to the Kingdom and told her to stop sinning. Jesus dined with prostitutes and tax collectors and did the same with them. He invited the condemned criminal on the cross next to His own to join Him in Paradise. This suggests to me that He would also call today's most vilified group of people—homosexuals—to walk with Him into new life.

I feel Jesus is instructing me to worship with both sinner and saint on Sunday morning; mow my neighbor's yard on Monday afternoon; dine with my students on Tuesday's Taco Day; and pray that all of them will catch a glimpse of who Jesus is in my words and actions.

14—what did Jesus promise?

Christ's Response to Our Uncertainty and Confusion

The Scripture

"If you love me, you will obey what I command. And I will ask the Father, and he will give you another counselor to be with you forever—the Spirit of truth. The world cannot accept him, because it neither sees him nor knows him. But you know him, for he lives with you and will be in you. I will not leave you as orphans; I will come to you. Before long, the world will not see me anymore, but you will see me. Because I live, you also will live. On that day, you will realize that I am in my Father, and you are in me, and I am in you. Whoever has my commands and obeys them, he is the one who loves me. He who loves me will be loved by my Father, and I too will love him and show myself to him."

Then Judas (not Judas Iscariot) said, "But Lord, why do you intend to show yourself to us and not to the world?"

Jesus replied, "If anyone loves me, he will obey my teaching. My Father will love him, and we will come to him and make our home with him. He who does not love me will not obey my teaching. These words you hear are not my own; they belong to the Father who sent me.

"All this I have spoken while still with you. But the Counselor, the Holy Spirit, whom the Father will send in my name, will teach you all things and will remind you of everything I have said to you. Peace I leave with you; my peace I give you" (John 14:15-27).

So I say, live by the Spirit, and you will not gratify the de-

sires of the sinful nature. For the sinful nature desires what is contrary to the Spirit, and the Spirit what is contrary to the sinful nature. They are in conflict with each other, so that you do not do what you want. But if you are led by the Spirit, you are not under law.

The acts of the sinful nature are obvious: sexual immorality, impurity and debauchery; idolatry and witchcraft; hatred, discord, jealousy, fits of rage, selfish ambition, dissensions, factions and envy; drunkenness, orgies, and the like. I warn you, as I did before, that those who live like this will not inherit the kingdom of God.

But the fruit of the Spirit is love, joy, peace, patience, kindness, goodness, faithfulness, gentleness and self-control (Gal. 5:16-23).

The Discussion

Jesus was 100 percent divine.

He was also 100 percent human.

These two statements conclude, then, that Jesus was—and is—the only "200 percent" being ever. Because of the latter, He died as all humans do, but because of the former, he lives eternally at the right hand of God as our holy "brother." Before He ascended into heaven, He comforted His followers with many promises, the greatest being that though they would no longer see "God, the Son" with their eyes, they would see "God, the Spirit" with their hearts.

Years later, Paul interpreted what this holy presence meant in practical, everyday terms to the church in Galatia. Whereas the world teaches selfishness and gratification, he wrote, the Holy Spirit teaches selflessness and genuine goodness. Instead of jealousy and discord, followers of Christ are to display patience and peace. This, then, is the final conclusion to be drawn when asking the question, "What would Jesus do?"

Paul's critics, and they were legion, claimed that he was not one of the original apostles and, therefore, did not have the authority to remove Judaic "law" from the requirements of conversion that had been practiced since the Old Testament. Paul answered them with one simple word: "grace." According to Paul, man's conversion has nothing to do with "works of the law"; rather, redemption is a gift from God that can never be earned by what a person does or says. Justification comes only through grace and one's faith in Christ's love, not through adherence to humankind's misguided legalism (*The NIV Study Bible,* 1779).

The Bottom Line

According to Scripture, a person's overriding motive in every decision, every action, and every utterance should be love—love that "does not boast, . . . is not proud, . . . is not rude, . . . is not self-seeking, . . . is not easily angered, . . . keeps no record of wrongs, . . . does not delight in evil [and] . . . never fails" (1 Cor. 13:4-6, 8). Indeed, the love of which Scripture speaks is a love that "is patient, . . . is kind, . . . rejoices with the truth, . . . protects, . . . trusts, . . . hopes [and] . . . perseveres" (vv. 4, 6-7). This is *agape,* self-sacrificial love, the kind of love that lays down its life for another.

Several years ago, a pastor told his congregation one of the profound truths of the Christlike lifestyle: in order to be like Jesus, one should treat everyone he or she meets as if that other person were Jesus himself. In other words, when confronted with a decision of behavior, simply imagine that the other person involved is Jesus. When you ask, "Should I give my last $20 to that panhandler over there?" imagine that panhandler is Jesus. When you see someone stranded with a flat tire on a neighboring street, picture Jesus in that car, needing a hand. When you spot a lonely widow sitting on a park bench, envision her as Jesus. Once you do, you will immediately ask *Him* if *He* would accept your help or company.

Second, according to Gal. 5, the attitude of a person who lives with the love of Christ should be *joyful.* This is not that kind of artificial, fake smile we sometimes wear so people think we're happy; this is sincere *joie de vivre* that comes from the hope of living with Jesus, both in the here-and-now and in the there-and-then. This is joy that comes when we realize that the trials of this life are only temporary and the temptations of this life are merely transient. It's the kind of happiness we associate with anticipation of wonderful things.

Remember the weeks before Christmas morning when you were a kid? You couldn't wait for that day to arrive: the tinseled tree, the colorfully wrapped gifts, the carols, the grandmas and grandpas, the uncles and aunts and cousins, the homemade fudge, the stockings, the laughter. You became so full of glee, you thought you might explode. You couldn't wait to talk to anyone who would listen about the traditions and expectations. That's the kind of joy the Scripture is trying to describe. It's as if life could not get any better!

Third, the state of being that love and joy bring to one's soul is *peace*. This is the ultimate sense of contentment, a true serenity of spirit the wisdom of which aligns all aspects of life in proper perspective and priority. It's the deep recognition that "this and that," "these and those" things don't really matter; in fact, only my willingness to give away "this and that," "these and those" things really matters.

I'm the first to admit that I have no idea how a car actually works. All I know is that it's supposed to start when I turn the key, take me to where I need to go, and stop when I press on the brake pedal. Other than that, I'm clueless. Recently, my car has been starting fine and stopping on cue, but it has chugged miserably as I've attempted to go from point A to point B. The ride is anything but peaceful. I suspect I know what the problem is because I had a 1963 Mercury Comet a few years ago that did the same thing. Turned out, the problem was a bad spark plug wire that kept popping off the spark plug.

I learned then that the four or six or eight spark plugs in

a car engine are supposed to fire in a prescribed order and if one of those plugs or wires gets "fouled" or out of sequence, the engine will buck like a 1,000-pound bull at a Friday night rodeo. Things are out of alignment, out of order. But when the master mechanic puts in new plugs and places the wires in the right sequence, that engine will purr like a well-fed kitten. Likewise, when our priorities are straight and we live the way the Master intended us to live, we are overwhelmed with a sense of profound peace.

Fourth, the life of a Christian is characterized by *patience,* also called "forbearance" or "tolerance." But patience is possible only when a person views his or her life through the lenses of love, joy, and peace—and not until.

I'm a Type A personality, which is pop-psychology's excuse for why I'm so hard to live with. I'm also compulsive-obsessive and a neatnik of the worst kind. I don't like anything out of place, I don't like anyone being late, and I don't want anything I own to break, leak, run down, go bad, or simply die of old age. I want my part of the world to run smoothly and on time, and left unchecked, I will do just about anything to make sure it is so. What that means is that I have a desperately hard time with lines of people waiting at the grocery store, slow assemblers at Taco Bell, red lights, snarled traffic, boring commercials, Daylight Savings Time, dead batteries, and anything else that doesn't fit my definition of life as I want it to be. That's my nature.

So when I read in the Bible that the life of a Christian is to be patient, I want to pray, "Lord, give me patience and give it to me *now.*" What has helped me over the years is the realization that first, I am not the center of the universe; and second, I need to put my feet in the other guy's shoes once in a while. When I want to lash out at someone for violating my rules, if I pause and ask myself, "What is that guy going through today?" I really calm down almost immediately. Chances are quite good, I've discovered, that he's having a worse day than I am and could really use a kind word or a helping hand. Then, when I follow through and say something nice to him or help him out of his jam, I feel so much better. You might say, I feel peaceful.

Fifth (and boy, does this follow nicely), another by-product of living the way Christ lived is being *kind* to people. This is a lot easier than we tend to think it is. Let's face it— when we lie in bed at night and replay some of the events of our day, don't most of us recognize that our impatience, loss of joy, or unkindness was due to being in a hurry because of unrealistically high self-expectations? Hey, we claim, we'd be *at peace* if we just had more time: a 26-hour day or an eight-day week. Or both.

There's a standard joke that runs through most professors' offices at most universities on most days: "Wow! I sure could get a lot more work done if it weren't for all these students." When we begin to put our work ahead of the people we work with—or even the people we work *for*—we tend to get short-tempered instead of long-suffering.

Sixth, when confronted with the question, "What would Jesus do?" the answer is always, "Something good." Genuine *goodness,* like kindness, is a state of mind that allows me to put others ahead of myself. In the next chapter of Galatians, Paul says, "as we have opportunity, let us do good to all people" (6:10). You can't believe how fun this can be!

One of my favorite things to do is to pay the toll for the car behind me, whether I'm on a bridge or a turnpike. I just love the idea of someone pulling up to the booth, disgruntled and mad, muttering horrible things about the unfairness of life, being charmed by the attendant with the most unexpected greeting ever: "Good morning. Your toll has already been paid, sir. You may proceed." One of my students told the class one day that one of his favorite things to do is to pay the bill for the car behind him at a drive-through restaurant. I even had a student whose tuition was paid one semester by an unnamed donor, which made my little toll-donation seem like nothing!

We learn this lesson slowly in life, but we learn it surely: it is a lot more fun to give than it is to get—just like on Christmas morning. It's too bad we don't take that sense of goodness to the other 364 days of the year, isn't it?

Seventh, Christ was *faithful*. Another way of saying this is that Christ was *consistent*. He was a man of *integrity*. He *put his money where his mouth was*. He *walked the talk*. He *practiced what He preached*. In order to be like Christ, then, we must live a life that not only is honest and forthcoming but also is honest and forthcoming every day in every situation. In order to be faithful, we must be constant and unwavering.

Many have misinterpreted this fruit of the Spirit as "faithfulness to the church"—that we must be in church whenever the doors are open and pay exactly 10 percent of our income, teach a Sunday School class and sing in the choir, wear a dress or tie and take the pastor out to dinner once a year. Though there's nothing inherently wrong in doing those things, certainly, that's a rather legalistic approach to the idea of fidelity. Faithfulness is complete allegiance to an idea or entity (in this context, a divine ethos) and a steadfast assurance of its truth.

Eighth, in order to be like Jesus, our bearing should be *gentle,* but this can only come through the peace of our faith and the hope of eternal residence with God, the Almighty.

Some of the gentlest people I know are those who are secure with themselves, not in the sense of accomplishment or material wealth, but in their certainty of what they believe. They're not caught up in the "me first" mentality of today's culture; they're centered on service to others. On the other hand, some of the harshest and severest people I know are those who have to be right or win all the time in order to feel good about themselves. They don't have time to be gentle; they have to be Number One. Gentle people have that wise ability to see *the big picture,* whereas dour folks seem to focus in on minutia.

Finally, one who calls himself or herself a *Christ-ian* exercises *self-control*. This is solely a matter of willpower that tames our emotions, tempers our desires, and reins in our actions so that we can, indeed, be persons of kindness, gentleness, and patience. Interestingly, it is kindness, gentleness, and patience that, in turn, breed self-control, isn't it? They all go hand-in-hand.

After his suffering, he showed himself to these men and gave many convincing proofs that he was alive. He appeared to them over a period of forty days and spoke about the kingdom of God. On one occasion, while he was eating with them, he gave them this command: "Do not leave Jerusalem, but wait for the gift my Father promised, which you have heard me speak about. For John baptized with water, but in a few days you will be baptized with the Holy Spirit."

So when they met together, they asked him, "Lord, are you at this time going to restore the kingdom to Israel?"

He said to them: "It is not for you to know the times or dates the Father has set by his own authority. But you will receive power when the Holy Spirit comes on you; and you will be my witnesses in Jerusalem, and in all Judea and Samaria, and to the ends of the earth."

After he said this, he was taken up before their very eyes,and a cloud hid him from their sight (Acts 1:3-9).